Too Much UnConvenience
Recollections of a Blues Gypsy

by Lincoln T. Beauchamp, Jr.
"Chicago Beau"

with
J. LaBosse

L. T. Beauchamp Publishing
Kansas City, Missouri

Too Much UnConvenience
by Lincoln T. Beauchamp, Jr.
ISBN 978-0-944602-00-3

Library of Congress
LCCN 2017902435

First Edition

Copyright 2016, Lincoln T. Beauchamp, Jr.
L. T. Beauchamp Publishing
6320 Brookside Plaza
Suite 153
Kansas City, Missouri 64113
www.chicagobeau.net

All rights reserved. No part of this publication may be reproduced, distributed, or transmitted in any form or by any means, including photocopying, recording, or other electronic or mechanical methods, without the prior written permission of the publisher, except in the case of brief quotations embodied in critical reviews and certain other non-commercial uses permitted by copyright law. For permission requests, write to the publisher, addressed "Attention: Permissions Coordinator," at the address above.

Cover photo: Ásta Magnúsdóttir
Inside photos: Beauchamp family archives

Disclaimer: This book is a combination of facts about the life of Lincoln T Beauchamp, Jr., and certain embellishments. I have tried to recreate events, locales and conversations from my memories of them. In order to maintain their anonymity in some instances I have changed the names of individuals and places, I may have changed some identifying characteristics and details such as physical properties, occupations and places of residence. The reader should not consider this book anything other than a work of literature. L. T. B.

Acknowledgements

LaBosse and I have been meeting, and having phone conversations about this memoir since 2012. Straight away, from me, and on behalf of the many people who have been a part of my life: LaBosse, thanks for being accessible, inspiring; and for being a co-conspirator, sharing many of my experiences. And merci mille fois to MiZsa LaBosse for your translations, critiques, and for traveling with LaBosse to our meetings.

Lillian Selonick, a wise young friend, who is a radio host, writer, and world traveler, thoroughly scrutinized early drafts of this project. Lillian's valuable opinions were encouraging, insightful, and confirm that Too Much UnConvenience is a work for all generations. Lillian! Thank you!

I am grateful to Dr. Sarah Tyrrell for her time and energy. Because of Sarah's brilliance and precision, this project reached completion. Sarah, I'm looking forward to teaming up again, and again. Obrigada Muito!

Many thanks to Ásta Magnúsdóttir for cover photo from the 2016 Reykjavik Blues Festival. Brava!

Immense gratitude to A. C. McGraw for her portrait of J. LaBosse. Always steadfast!

Foreward

I was honored by the invitation to edit these chapters and proud to play some small part in the collaboration that will bring the book to print.

I sense that this story is important on many fronts. It goes without saying that it is much more than a narrative about a particular segment of one man's life—and that its reach will extend far beyond that of a myopic autobiography. Instead, Beau's words remind readers that we are all born with a spirit of adventure—and with the free will to see that adventure through. More importantly, probably, is that in reading this, Beau's deliberate intentions to move, to progress, to learn, and to explore get into one's head: I'm left feeling obligated to get going on my own pilgrimage. Beau has re-instilled in me something I'm sure I knew at one time in my life: that everyone is charged with cultivating and indulging that singular dimension of self that screams, "Go!" We are each responsible for imagining and then creating our own destinies.

Ultimately, too, the story affirms that while life with fewer boundaries might render rich rewards, the point is never to erase those lines, or to ignore differences inherent to region, culture, race, and language. Instead, Beau proves the point that we should recognize, confront, and respect—taking whatever value we can from a life carefully crafted through travel, curiosity, wonder, and awareness.

Enjoy the forthright honesty in these pages because the essence of his story indeed holds merit—not toward sensationalizing events or idealizing experiences, but in how Beau puts into sharp relief the polarizing dualities and alternative forces of his time.

Sarah Tyrell, Kansas City, Missouri

Table of Contents

Acknowledgements
iii

Foreward
iv

Introductions
Thoughts on Too Much UnConvenience
by DonAlonzo Beauchamp
vi

On Friendship with Chicago Beau
by J. LaBosse
ix

Dedication
xiii

Hotel Glöcklhofer Cafe Lounge
1

Ritz Carlton, Chicago
DECA Bar and Cafe
37

Chez J. F. Fabiano
Sainte-Saveur-des-Monts, Québec
99

Hilton Nordica, Reykjavik Blues Festival
135

Photograhs
162

Thoughts on Too Much UnConvenience
by DonAlonzo Beauchamp

What an honor it is to have the opportunity to write about Chicago Beau, who has been a tremendous influence on my life. I first met Beau when I was around seven years old, and little did I know that my life would be changed forever. He shared a very loving friendship and marriage with my mother and became a father to me in many ways during my formative years. He has a way of expressing joy in life with all things and inspired a spirit of adventure in me at a young age. It is through this spirit that I was able to develop the courage to explore the world, pursue my destiny, and experience a charmed life filled with music, love, and the Spirits of the Ancestors by honoring the journey as opposed to the destination.

This book is presented as a memoir, but really only represents the tip of the iceberg of the wealth of stories and experiences that I have been fortunate enough to have heard. Beau paints a very complete and thorough picture of his upbringing and childhood to provide insights into how the Last Saboom Boom Gypsies came to be. He delves into his childhood life with family and school with incredible detail in order to give a very vivid foundation of the formation of a Blues life in 1960s Chicago, which may be contradictory to what many may assume. Because of his Blues Experience, perspectives that otherwise would go unnoticed come into focus in a larger cultural picture. Beau modernizes the Blues as an educated, literate, and critical thinking product of prominent Black life, as opposed to the stereotypical "Bluesman" image of a downtrodden product of oppression and poverty. Through this, he is able to put into context the climate that propelled his ability and desire to embark on an incredible journey which allowed him to expand his experiences beyond a normal urban life that limits so many, not only in the sixties, but today as well.

A pioneer in the path of adventure for the generations coming of age during the Civil Rights movement, his travels led him to Boston, Canada, Europe, and beyond. He is never looking back, always trusting in the "Beacons of the Cosmics" to forge the path forward. He tells of chance meetings that blossomed into steadily guiding forces, always moving on his road to discovery and adventure. This road took Beau to Europe where he could really develop the identity that would define him and his place in the history of Black music, literature, and art as life.

First London, then Paris, and just about everywhere else in Europe, Beau was able to navigate the right circles as a black American artist in the sixties since there was such an excitement about Black American culture ongoing at that time. Of course, the navigation of these circles can be challenging, and in many ways this book serves as a survival guide for the adventurer/artist. He describes several dealings with artists, dancers, poets, writers, and publishers, and he sets the stage for what ultimately allowed him to establish himself as all of those things. These stories are intertwined with accounts of some of the relationships with ladies, philanthropists, and supporters of the arts who led to some of these dealings, all of which provide for entertaining reading.

Beau fell in love and that brings another dynamic to the story entirely. As the book continues, the adventures don't stop, but rather take on new shapes through his relationship with his first wife, Linda, and mother of his first child, Jessica. The love does not last, but the unswerving, greater, binding, soul-to-soul love of friendship remains strong. He continued his journey to new places and deemed to have perfected the art of navigating special scenes from Rome, Greece, and up to Scandinavia, somehow able to land in the right scenes with the right people by sticking to fundamentals of trusting the Cosmics.

The book fast-forwards to Beau's return to Chicago after being back in the states for a few years mostly on the West coast, where he met and married his second wife, Rose, my mother. This was somewhat of an uneventful period musically, but it laid the foundation for his emergence as a literary publisher and development of Literati Chicago and Original Chicago Blues Annual with his third wife, A.-C. Mc Graw.

Back in Chicago, much older and established, he was able to develop the relationships necessary to run his publishing company for several years. He expands into music to form a production company, Straight Ahead Productions, producing Chicago Blues musicians through DIW Records of Tokyo and co-producing concerts and recordings in Iceland and Sardegna.

In 1994, feeling the need for a shift in energy and environment, Beau relocates his residence to Montreal, while continuing to produce events and publications in the U.S. and abroad; however, in 1996 he decided to become semi-reclusive in Tuscany for a few months. Afterwards, he moved to Rome for four years where he indulged himself to the fullest in the pleasures of Roman lifestyle. It was in his Roman period that he wrote the now collectible book, Great Black Music – The Art Ensemble of Chicago. And it was in Tuscany that he met Dooney O'Neill; they married in Reykjavik in 2001. Later that year, Beau, Dooney, and her sons, Luca and Raffy, moved to the Algarve for four years. Their daughter, Beguine, was born in Faro in 2003.

These chapters of Beau's recollections close with him returning to Chicago and eventually embarking on yet another adventure, The Chicago Blues Experience, a cultural institution for the city of Chicago and for the world. What an appropriate name for what may be the flagship achievement of the Last of The Sa Boom Boom Gypsies, Chicago Beau, the man who lived, cultivated, and helped redefine what is The Chicago Blues Experience. Ashé

DonAlonzo Beauchamp, April, 2009, Helsinki, Finland

J. LaBosse on Friendship with Chicago Beau

I was born in 1934. I feel good, but a touch of arthritis exists in my fingers making it difficult to type or to write in longhand for more than a few minutes at a sitting. I knew it would be difficult to even write briefly about my relationship with my dear friend, Beauchamp, so I have enlisted the help of another dear friend, my brilliant and loving wife, MiZsa. I am speaking to her in French, and she translates into her own style of French-based English, that I quite admire, as we move along.

I was born in Martinique; however, my mother was from Panama and as is the case of my father, her exact origins are unknown. They are descended from the enslaved African labour force that was brought to the Caribbean during the past four hundred years. I never met my father.

As a young man, I found work in the bowels of a French freighter. For a few years, I lived in Marseille, often travelling to North Africa and Paris. I attended a rather nondescript lycée near Marseille where my only notable endeavour was creating an organization, *Le Bottoms Up Société des Hérétiques,* which didn't sit well with the school administration. Afterwards, I attended the Sorbonne for two years.

Ladies of all social strata found me witty, attractive, and engaging, so being dangerously too self-absorbed, I became a dandy of the boulevards, frolicking and fondling throughout the first, fifth, eighth, sixteenth, and seventeenth arrondissements, with unrestrained dalliances in Pigalle. And as one of my admirers put it, I was a young man of "piercing intellect" ready to dive into the most intense discussions ranging from soccer to existentialism.

And in those days, it was not difficult to meet and engage well-known public and beloved figures like Jean-Paul Sartre and Josephine Baker. All one really had to do was to visit ex-Chicagoan Leroy Haynes' Restaurant at 3 Rue Clauzel, and there, as I did, encounter people like Richard Wright, Nina Simone, Sydney Bechet, Cab Calloway, James Baldwin, and countless others. Paris was happening. In my opinion, those days were the beginning of the end of the *Belle Epoch.*

I was a naturally gifted piano player and would dazzle the patrons at some of the salons and private clubs I attended with my own interpretation of pieces like Prokofiev's Piano Concerto Number 1, or Duke Ellington's *In a Sentimental Mood*. It was music that would eventually lead to me meeting young Beauchamp.

In 1965 I travelled to the United States to experience live performances of blues and jazz in its *rootland*, and to whenever possible play with roots masters. I had a minor traffic accident in Chicago, and because I had a foreign driver's licence, spoke not very good English, and was driving a borrowed car registered to a white person, which was evident because of the address, I was taken to a police station for questioning. An attorney overheard my difficult discussion with the Chicago police and offered his assistance. He passed me his business card. It read Lincoln T. Beauchamp, Attorney at Law, 417 E. 47th Street, Chicago, Illinois. I was released from the police station after my story had been verified with the assistance of Attorney Beauchamp, who was well known by the police.

The next day I went to see Mr. Beauchamp at his office, after hours. I later learned that for him there was no such thing as "after hours," as he worked tirelessly into the night on a regular basis. When I arrived, the secretary had gone for the day, and the person occupying that seat was Mr. Beauchamp's son, Lincoln Jr. Mr. Beauchamp was with a client in his inner office. There was another person in the waiting room whom I recognized from album covers and concerts I had attended. That person was pianist Ahmad Jamal. I was moved: Jamal had been a client of Mr. Beauchamp for years. I learned that many in the music business had retained the services of Mr. Beauchamp. On another occasion, in fact, the last time I saw Mr. Beauchamp, I met Eddie Thomas, manager of The Impressions singing group and of Curtiss Mayfield.

In speaking with the younger Beauchamp, I was reminded in many way of myself. He was a dreamer. And at that age, he was convinced of certain processes to make things happen– things that it takes many people decades, if at all, to grasp. An axiom as old as time was at the basis of his thinking: *Imagine it, then make it happen*. And with that he told of his vision of being an adventurer, writer, and, "Lord knows, the recipient of the unending bounty of the unknown," is exactly how he put it. I shared selected stories of my own with him while Jamal was in with Mr. Beauchamp. I was careful not to share anything too revealing with a young man that age. I mostly focused on my youth, travels, and my intention of continuing the same. He was around sixteen, and was in my opinion, a most unusual person, but still a minor . . . my lawyer's young son.

Lincoln Junior worked for his father as an all-around law clerk that included paralegal work, serving summonses, typing, etcetera. Around two years after our initial meeting, Lincoln came across my file in his father's filing cabinets. He wrote down all my contact information: Paris, Martinique, Montreal, and Madagascar. He sent letters to all of them with return addresses in Québec City and Boston.

Over time all of his letters arrived at their destinations. I received the one sent to Montreal within a month of its writing. Young Beauchamp was in Québec City, and after many attempts, we spoke by telephone and arranged to meet at a café near the Expo '67 World's Fair taking place in Montreal. I was there doing my thing, having a ball with the ladies, but that's another story that can be told by Beauchamp at another time if he chooses.

We met. I revealed more of my life, and he shared his aspirations and plans. I told him not to be impressed with me, because like all people, regardless of their vision, there will always be struggles and surprises, some not pleasant. It's best at times to put everything in the hands of the Cosmics, our Ancestors, then roll on, then dream on.

As time moves on, relationship roles can level off, then reverse. In today's world, I look to Chicago Beau to advise me on certain matters like changes within cultures, the relevance of social mores, music, technology, and much more. I'm fifteen years his senior, and he is still in the mix.

This book, *Too Much UnConvenience*, could have been approached in several different ways. The conversation format is at Beau's insistence. He wanted an ear, and as he spoke, I realized the importance of listening, responding, and prompting. There is a lot more that can been said and will be said. I hope you enjoy, laugh, maybe grimace, or shout, but ultimately benefit in some way from our conversations.

Peace and Music to All!

J. LaBosse avec MiZsa, 13 Mars, 2017, Bora Bora

Portrait of J. LaBosse by A. C. McGraw

Dedication
For Family, Elders, Ancestors, Cosmics

Ancestor, Golden 'Big' Wheeler: thanks for your constant encouragement.

So sad to be lonesome, and it's too much unconvenient to be alone.
                                                        Sonny Boy Williamson

Baron-la-Croix #15

I am Baron-la-Croix
The dog that howls at death
In your garden is me
The Black moth
That flies about the table is me
One word too many and I'll transform
Your little southern lives
Into as many crosses
Forged in the iron of my soul!
            From *Epiphanies of Voodoo Gods*, René Depestre

"My uncles: 'Boy, don't ever kiss no pussy. I mean that, whatever you do in life, don't kiss no pussy!' I couldn't wait to kiss a pussy. They'd been wrong about everything else!"
                                                        Richard Pryor

Too Much Unconvenience

Hotel Glöcklhofer
Cafe Lounge
Burghausen JazzWoche
Burghausen, Germany
17 March, 2013

LaBosse: Beau, thanks for inviting me here to Burghausen. Your performance yesterday was brilliant, and the band... smokin'. It was good to see drummer Sam Kelly again. I haven't seen him since you guys played at the Half Note in Athens back in 2002. We've been talking about working on your memoir-as-interview since forever it seems. Hey, here we are, and I'm ready to get down with you and get your stories told. Are you ready—are you feelin' good?

Beau: Thanks, LaBosse. I'm feeling good, and I'm definitely ready. You're looking well also. You've always been sharp dresser. . . one for the ladies. I like that Stetson you're sporting. If there is such a style as Venetian Creole, that's you.

Yeah, man. I got the look for where I've been moving around. It-fits. I'm between Venice, Montreal, and Panama City, where I've been spending a lot of time lately. And really, my brother, you should get out of cold-ass Chicago before you lose your tropical flow, and the politics of separation, inequality, and urban gloom suck out your *joie de vivre*.

Soon, soon. I will be on the move again.

All right. Here we are. From where in your life would you like to begin your recollections?

With some earliest memories. Generally, unless something culturally or politically significant or scandalous, or deep hardship happened, a kid's life can be rather mundane. But that does not include child soldiers and victims of all sorts of abuse. Their stories should never be suppressed, in order for the world to step up and fight exploitation of children and misery worldwide. You've known me for decades and you know many of my choices have been directly related to the way I was raised. They've been often guided by my parents' resistance to the status quo. My parents came from agrarian backgrounds, and contrary to the post-Reconstruction plan to suppress Blacks, they could out-think, out-perform their oppressors and thrive in a racist and hostile American environment. I will speak about my parents and their upbringing early on, sometimes interspersed with other stories. You and I should keep in mind that this book a lengthy conversation between us combined with *Griot* storytelling tradition. The typical guidelines of the literary establishment have no priority here. Their guidelines are for themselves and those that prefer them. You know, the way Euro-centric thinking works is that somethings are considered unorthodox, or even unacceptable until they figure out how to profit from it. That's the case with marijuana: now it's gradually becoming legal and generating enormous profits. Prescription and street drugs abuse is now treated as an illness, and the users need rehab and therapy, generating money for that profession and associated therapeutic drugs. And Billie Holiday and Gene Ammons, and the countless others who got high and were harassed by the police or rotted in prisons, you dig? And with the Blues, it was once the called "Devil's music." In a way, black artists being cheated out of rights and royalties is devilish, but that's not the way they meant it. So, the key here is conducting our converstion on our own terms and not altering it to please or seek approval from those that ain't got nothing to do with our culture and experiences. As Gore Vidal wisely stated: "It's about knowing who you are, what you want to say, and not giving a damn."

Well said. Earliest recollections that stand out? Come on, break it on down!

There are many. As a child I had a continuous confirming inner voice that would shout, or sometimes whisper, or sometimes just be a sensation that went: *This is who you are, this is what you feel. Fear not.* I've never fought that. And so throughout, there are stories within stories, and stories that segue into other stories; their relevance is subjective. Some behavior is impulsive and fun. They are personality and sensitivity-shaping. My plan is not to adhere to a strict chronology of events, but to ebb and flow, pivot, step up, fall back, leap forward, and maybe do the verbal Uncle Willie, a dance of words.

I was born in 1949. I remember being less than two years old. I have clear images of rolling around in my baby crib when we lived on Oakwood Boulevard between Drexel Boulevard and Lake Park Avenue, just up the street from the infamous Green Gables Hotel, Murdering Two Gun Pete's, Hill Top Lounge, and the Blue Flame Blues Club. I was crawling and toddling around, getting into things, observing what was going on in the house. It was not our house. My parents rented a room in the home of a lady by the name of Mrs. Terrell. She was one of those people who seemed ageless. She looked the same to me when I was a teenager as she did when I was I was a toddler: dark skin, white curly hair, pleasant, yet an in-charge manner. I don't recall her first name. I probably never heard it called. In those days people often referred to older people, or people in a position of authority such as a landlady or landlord as Mr. or Mrs. That was considered good manners. The house was exciting, full of activity and music. There was always music playing, either78's on the record player or music on the radio. Mrs. Terrell had stacks of blues and jazz records. I remember seeing the RCA and Bluebird labels that produced Race Records back then, so I got an earful of Duke Ellington, Earl Hines, Ruby Smith, Coleman Hawkins, bluesy Count Basie, and others. Of course, at that time it was just music to me; however, I mention Basie's bluesyness because even as a child I was moved more by his music more than the other big bands. After I got older and visited the Terrell's with my parents, I began to recognize the significance of the music.

I later learned that Mrs. Terrell's tall and lanky dope-head son, Bill, was a numbers runner. I remember the betting slips, dream books, and sharply dressed ladies and gentlemen that would drop by and hang out around the kitchen table. Some of them cats were old-time Zoot Suiters. Decked out! Now and then somebody would hit The Numbers. Man, they would jump up and down, dance the Jitterbug, start hugging and kissing. Some ladies would lift their skirts just above their knees and do the squat dance. Oh yeah, when somebody hit—big, big fun! I was swept up by the atmosphere and would start dancing.

These were the early stages, or building blocks for your forth coming passion for living and fun?

Yes, hanging around in the kitchen was wildness foundation building. I was slightly shorter than the height of the table, which meant that I had a great view under the dresses of the ladies seated at the table. Even though I was only a toddler, something inside me said playing between and rubbing against perfumed ebony thighs was a good thing, especially since the ladies didn't seem to mind. And this was before the widespread popularity of pantyhose, so the ladies' private areas were not hidden behind layers of fabric. They generally wore garter belts, and sometimes a garter belt attached to a girdle, which was the least appealing. And some didn't have on no drawz at all. Ever since then I've always had a thing for skirts and thighs.

How did it feel getting attention from the ladies?

I think what I felt, even though I was a toddler, was maybe...pre-sexual, as in stirrings "down in my down-down," as the folks used to say. There was something arousing and comforting about being close to women in that way, and yet I didn't have an erection. It was an inner warmth and deeply personal feeling. The scent of women gave me a wonderful sensation. I was always looking for an opportunity to be close to women, between their legs if I could. That pattern has always been a part of me. I was never the kind of man that wanted to be "one of the fellas." I liked being around girls! I can't even begin to comprehend the idea of a man cave.

Were your parents aware of your feelings?

I think they became aware as I got older, as my sense of humor early on often included sexual innuendo, and I took advantage of any opportunity to be close to the ladies. I was around four when we moved from Mrs. Terrell's house into our own apartment at 848 E. 40th Street in 1953. My parents occasionally invited friends over for Sunday dinner. On this one occasion Mr. and Mrs. S. were seated on the sofa. Mr. S. was engrossed in conversation with my father and Mrs. S. was talking with me as I squirmed around in front of her on the floor. I had never seen a woman like her before. I had never seen a white woman before in person, let alone had the opportunity to look under her skirt. In fact, I hadn't started noticing race at that age. Her whiteness just seemed different. Here is this woman from Denmark. She is statuesque with fine legs, wearing no underwear. Every time she shifts this way or that way I get a great view. I was looking straight at her pussy, and that was profoundly arousing, nearly intoxicating. I knew nothing about sexual acts, but I knew I wanted to kiss her. I wanted to kiss everything that she was showing me. Everything!. And I wanted to kiss what I couldn't see, but just imagined. Entire booty. In retrospect, I believe she was exhibiting herself on purpose, and surely derived pleasure from this exhibition, which was, of course, undetectable by the others present. And just like with the ladies at Mrs. Terrell's, I tried to snuggle between her thighs, but this time there was no table for me to hide under. My mother walked into the room and saw me playing around her legs. She went back into the kitchen, ordering me to come there immediately. I hesitated just a few seconds too long. "Boy, I said come in here, now!" Again, I hesitated, so she came and got me by the arm. I was inconsolable. I screamed, kicked, threw myself on my bed, and cried and cried. What I was feeling was total humiliation. My dad and Mr. S. continued their conversation, hardly noticing my tantrum. However, my mother was surely aware of what was going on in my head. From that day forth there was never another opportunity for me to look under a skirt in her presence.

Interesting, Mrs. S. has stuck in your mind?

Yeah, she was fine. Besides them hot legs, she had an exquisite protruding booty. I used to just imagine would it might look like. I still get a buzz from recollecting. Ha-ha! About a week after this incident, I had a dream about a booty that was recurring for about five years. Check this out: On a fall day, I am walking down Lake Park Avenue, south of 40th Street, with my mother at my right, on the west side of the street. Most of the houses are spacious frame houses with fallen leaves on the front yards. We are walking towards the house of the Turner family who we often visited. This was the home of my first friend, Rani. Rani's father, Dr. Lorenzo Dow Turner, was a famous linguist specializing in African languages and dialects spoken in the Americas directly linked to those languages. His work is extremely important and I will speak more about him and his work later. As I said, my mother and I are walking down the street when there comes into view two figures maybe fifty yards ahead of us, but I cannot make out what the figures are. Suddenly, our walking speed is accelerated as though we are being pushed along by the wind, but it's not frightening. I ask my mother if she feels it; she says no. As we close in on the two figures, I'm able to determine what they are. Floating, not walking, side-by-side, are a rust-colored monkey wrench about five feet tall and a huge, round, beige ass. The ass is in front of me, the monkey wrench is in front of my mother. The ass has no legs and no torso; it's just an ass, a pretty ass. My mother said nothing and stood expressionless as we were right behind the duo. I asked, "Who are you?" Then I heard an unfamiliar female voice coming from the ass saying, "I'm Dit-DehDeh, and he's Din-DaDur." As is often the case in dreams, one's perspective of things can change rapidly. I went from being behind the pair at a distance, to rubbing Deht-DehDeh across her crack and rubbing my face against her right cheek. Din-DaDur, the monkey wrench, abruptly cleared his throat as though he were annoyed. His monkey wrench head went up and down, clanking until his wrench mouth was completely closed. My mother was no longer in the dream, and then I awoke. I didn't tell my mother or father about the dream. I went to sleep many nights hoping to have the dream again, hoping to go further into the world of Deht-DehDeh and Din-DaDur. Then one night I'd have the dream again. But it never changed. There were no further adventures of Deht-DehDeh and Din-DaDur, but the dream was always pleasant.

What do you think the dream meant?

I must say this: I think that many dream interpreters are bullshitters. I've told no less than three of them, including a well-known psychoanalyst in Zurich, Dr. R.R., about the dream. Here are short versions of their interpretations. Theory Number One: I'm probably born gay and the pair symbolized my inborn desire for a strong male companion to replace my mother. That's why the monkey wrench cleared his throat when I rubbed my face against Deht-DehDeh. Theory Number Two: The monkey wrench was my father and the ass my mother. I must have a deep fear of my father so I sought protection from the ass. Theory Number Three from the guy in Zurich: I'm bi-sexual. The monkey wrench is a strong symbol of virility, and I probably see myself as a virile conqueror of women, but since Deht-DehDeh was only an ass without breasts or a vagina, I probably prefer men.

Here's my take on it: I was about five when I first had the dream. My mother never walked around me unclothed. However, at some point I must have certainly seen her ass, and she was fair complexioned. As for the monkey wrench, I remember seeing the apartment building janitor using one to fix some pipes. Every experience we have becomes a part of our memory and can become part of our dreams during sleep or half awake. Now let's bring in my genes. African men like big asses, and many Africans and their descendants generally have asses much larger than other ethnic groups. The only ass I may have seen was that of my mother. Not even my older sister's, who was always hiding and shouting "Don't peek" anyway. Black people are generally booty people. So, the dream was simply a combination things I had seen, genes, and my imagination, hence, Dhet-DehDeh and Din-DaDur. And yes, to this very day… lady asses. Gots to be… them African genes. But some psychologists are damn wacky themselves. The one who suggested that I may prefer men was looking at his own brain, as he did wiggle his eyebrows at me.

Are these just random thoughts popping into your head, or do you think about these things from time to time?

These are early recollections. Asked on a different day, you may get some different answers. Another strong memory I have is of painting over every single page in my sister's coloring book with black and blue watercolors.

Damn, why did you do that?

It was partially revenge because she was older, taller, and

would kick my ass any time she felt like it, which was often and partially just to see her reaction. I knew I was going to get a whuppin and that she would be out for revenge. But she was sneaky. She wasn't going to do anything right away. About a week later she asked me sweetly if I wanted a glass of milk before I went to bed. I ended up taking a big gulp out of a glass filled with hand lotion. I knew she was going to get into trouble for that. She got a medium whuppin. I could hear her hollering a bit, just enough for me to have a laugh.

Y'all got a lot of whuppins?

Not so many. The worst one I got was when I called my sister an ugly baboon. That really upset my mother. She whupped me down the hall and into the living room where I cringed underneath the piano. She whupped me so much that I stopped crying and started laughing. I was crying with laughter, and vice versa. I was glad when she stopped, but my sister was loving every crack of that strap. I couldn't get her back until years later when we lived on the West Side. I put muddy earthworms in her bed one day after a rainstorm. But then I just got yelled at.

Before we move on...?

I must say that outside of the usual nonsense that goes on between siblings, our home life was splendid. Yeah, we spent time living in a rooming house with all kind of stuff going on. And I know that it was a difficult adjustment for my parents. My mother grew up on a farm near Henderson, Kentucky. She was number ten of fourteen children, and they were not cramped up. She said they shared rooms in the house, but there was plenty of room to roam, and everybody around was family, not like all them wild, but caring people at Mrs. Terrell's. But those were Post-War days. My father got drafted into the Army at forty years old in 1943. He rushed and joined the Navy immediately with the hope of avoiding combat. That worked out okay; he was assigned to clerical work and personnel movement. His dream of having a continuous law practice got deferred. Now, you combine that with the struggles that went along with being black during that era, and brother, your life was challenging. My parents provided well. I could never say I was denied any necessity. Given the poor circumstances my agrarian parents came from in the South, the existence they provided, and the vision they had was nothing short of a marvel. They were used to struggle and challenges. And they gave their all so that my sister and I could grow up with a life of opportunity and possibilities.

My parents were into books. Reading was a daily activity in our household. My mother read to us nearly every day. As a toddler, she read me nursery rhymes, and even created and recalled fascinating stories in the oral tradition, talking about our ancestors. After we moved from Mrs. Terrell's, my parents quickly developed a library that included the *Encyclopedia Britannica*, *World Book Encyclopedia*, Childcraft Books, multiple volumes of Harvard Classics, and books by Harlem Renaissance writers Langston Hughes, Sterling Brown, Angelina Weld Grimké, W.E.B. DuBois, Zora Neal Hurston, and others. My mother had current and back issues of *The Crisis Magazine*, and John Johnson's *Jet* and *Ebony* magazines. We had the Chicago and *Louisville Defender* newspapers, and my mother insisted that my sister and I read them as we grew older. One day my dad brought Webster's Unabridged Dictionary; that was so huge that it required its own piece of furniture to sit on. My sister and I were interested in writing from early on. In fact, sister, Margaret, published a hep prose-poem, "Shadows," in the *Chicago Tribune* back in 1962. She was sixteen years old.

Would you say that your parents were a major influence on your literary endeavors?

Absolutely. My father was the first black graduate of John Marshall Law School in Chicago, class of 1932. My mother went to a post-reconstruction black college, Arkansas AM&N, in Pine Bluff, and had graduated in 1940. She had a part-time teaching job in Evanston, Illinois, shortly after college. Learning was fresh in her mind. She and my dad wanted us kids to have a solid learning foundation in preparation for this world. They taught us to think outside of the norm and sometimes, given the social and political environment in the United States, that was challenging.

How else did you parents prepare you?

My sister and I were given various lessons. Margaret studied ballet, music, and took French language classes with my dad. I studied music and tap dancing with legendary tap master Jimmy Payne. We both became very good figure skaters, having studied at the

Tower Cabana Club with renowned skater Melodee Hughes on Chicago's Northwest side.

Ice Skating. That certainly wasn't typical.

No, it wasn't. But, there has always been an abundance of creative talent in the black communities. There are lots of lessons taking place, and many black parents who want their children to learn, grow, and achieve. Of course, that's not what was presented by American media down through the years. It's a bit better today. Taking skating lessons at the Tower Cabana Club was not typical at all. It was on Peterson Avenue near Kedzie, in a solidly white neighborhood called Hollywood Park. My mother was a badass when she wanted something for her children. We may have been the only black people to set foot in the club, even in the neighborhood, unless it was for doing some type of domestic work. When my mother brought us for our first lesson, nearly everyone in the place had a look of shock on their faces, and some could be heard murmuring. She went to the registration, signed us up, paid the fees, and that was that. No one ever uttered a demeaning comment in the two years we took lessons and eventually appeared in ice shows. For a time, our family and Melodee Hughes' family enjoyed a wholesome friendship.

Your mother believed in breaking barriers?

Oh, yes. And it happened a lot with both of my parents. We were raised not to be afraid of white people or give them any undue respect just because they're white. We were taught to respect everyone as human, equal, and free, unless they proved to be otherwise. My mother also coached us about when, and when not, to display brilliance when dealing with certain Whites who hate Blacks that they feel are uppity or educated. This was deep south training, that, used in certain circumstances, could save your health or life. Most unfortunately, this resentment of black achievers is alive and thriving. The off-the-charts ignorant, racist comments about Venus and Serena Williams and the Obamas are examples.

More about your childhood surroundings and growing up.

The streets and shops of the neighborhood are still vivid in my mind. I recall the live poultry shop on Cottage Grove just south of Oakwood Boulevard where you picked your chicken, goose, or duck, and a few minutes later that bird was brought to you beheaded, de-feathered, wrapped in newspaper and ready for cooking. And there was Henry Glen's wooden newspaper shack on the southeast corner of Oakwood and Cottage Grove. I was privileged. I got to sit in his shack from time to time and hand newspapers out of a small sliding window to customers. I also got my first peeks at girlie magazines. Some of the newspapers don't exist today: the *Chicago Herald American* and the *Daily News* are long gone. The Cottage Grove streetcar line had its turn-around a block from our home in front of a five-and-dime store. There was a nickel Coca-Cola machine there that I got to drop money in and push the lever to get a bottle of Coke. This was before cans. Then you had the fruit and vegetable vendors who drove horse-drawn carts through the alleys. They would sing-shout: "Hey, hey! I got apples, watermelons, and big red peaches, onions, cabbage, and sweet potatoes!" Running down the back steps with my mother and father to hang with him was big fun, just patting the horse and listening to the vendor's humorous snippets about food and pretty women. He would say something to a young woman like, "Child, I knows you knows how to pick a good, long, firm sweet potato!" Everybody hanging around would crack-up. Sometimes a lady would blush, then grab a big sweet potato and wave it around. Lots of laughter. My father enjoyed those encounters as they reminded him of when he was a horse-cart driving street vendor when he first came to Chicago back in the twenties.

    One of my family's favorite activities was going for rides on public transportation, often riding various trains, buses, and streetcars to the end of the line. Back in those days the streetcars operated in downtown Chicago along State Street, and going down there in the 1950s was a real adventure. Most of the buildings between Van Buren and Lake Street are still there, but the businesses have changed several times. The big stores like Carson Pirie Scott, Mandel Brothers, and Marshall Field's each had a Toyland, which was paradise for my sister and me. I remember the creaking, wooden red streetcars with wicker seats were replaced with cream and green cars with leather seats. Sadly, and I think unwisely, electric ground transit has vanished in Chicago.

You've always said that you felt good to be going somewhere. I remember once you said, "Just point me in any direction, and

start rambling." Did getting around Chicago prompt you to want to travel beyond the city?

Oh, yeah, without a doubt. I was always asking my parents if we could go somewhere. I thought being any place else would be more exciting than where I was. For years before my father bought a car, which was in 1958, we took public transportation on local trips, and sometimes farther. We took a long-ass ride from 39th street on the South Side to Brookfield Zoo, which was all the way across the city in the western suburbs. The zoo trip took hours. In those days, there was not an "El" train going out to the West Side, and the Eisenhower Expressway had not yet been built. We took a streetcar downtown, then connected to an electric bus that ran down Roosevelt Road to the end of the line, then transferred to the Blue Bird bus that went to the zoo. Riding the Blue Bird bus was my favorite part of the journey because the bus had rows of two seats together on one side of the bus, and single seats on the other. I got to sit in a single seat, which gave me a feeling of independence. By the time we got home after an eight-hour day, we were all exhausted, and my mother was vowing, rather emphatically, never to endure another trip to the zoo. And a big drawback going to the zoo was the necessity to travel through the all-white western suburbs of Brookfield, Berwyn, and Cicero before dark. White people, police, and others were known to harass and sometimes attack Blacks. I remember once a black family moved to Cicero: it wasn't long before they were forced to leave. House set on fire. Of course, it's not that way today. But, from the seventies on back, it was terrible.

Another family trip was a ride on the South Shore train from Chicago to Gary, or South Bend, Indiana. I recall one Easter Sunday, we all dressed up and my father had arranged special seating through someone he knew. No one else in the coach but us and another family out on an outing, enjoying food and beverages. They were nice trains, but the train I liked the most was the North Shore *Electroliner* that went from Chicago to Milwaukee, and all the stops in between. It was a luxury train that had a bar and diner. They served wine, cocktails, and sandwiches and sold cigars, cigarettes, and various smokers requisites that included Zippo lighters, matches, cigar and cigarette holders. I was impressed with luxury at an early age. I was around five or six years old when we rode on these trains, and I was already developing an appreciation for quality service and luxury. There were few black people on these trains as passengers. We were never refused service by the white staff, but we certainly got looks and heard the occasional racist comment. My father loved it: taking the family out to the best restaurants, riding the best trains, and standing proudly as a non-kiss-ass black attorney who'd been through hell growing up in East Texas. He derived great pleasure seeing white people annoyed by his gentlemanly manner, well-dressed family, and cash to spend.

Their annoyance was a reaction to your independence and someone who was courteous, dignified, and black, right?

Exactly. And a lesson from my dad was to maintain your dignity, and don't lose your cool. Don't let the rage emerge.

Your dad inspired your urge to move around?

He did. Here is a something that happened when we lived on the West Side of Chicago. I did some potentially dangerous things. You see, during the summer I would go to day camp at the Sears YMCA that was located at Kedzie and Arthington. My mother would drop me off around 9am and pick me up around 4pm. The Y was a fun place: swimming, gymnastics, billiards, dances, and girls. But sometimes I would get bored and sneak off. There was no security or head-count. Kids came and went, and in those days, rarely did you hear about abductions or child molestation.

This is in 1959 and 1960, so I was ten and eleven years old. I would take the bus downtown. My destination was downtown to visit train stations. First, I would go to LaSalle Street Station and watch trains come and go: The New York Central and Pennsylvania lines were my favorites. I would talk with black workers at the station about trains. I became buddies with redcaps, Pullman porters, janitors, and shoeshine men.

Then I would go to Union Station, where I met a guy named Otis Jackson who cleaned the railroad cars. I just happened to meet him once while I was talking to the shoeshine man, and Mr. Jackson was getting a shine. He offered to walk me out to the railroad yards so that I could see the trains up close. Man, oh man, what a thrill that was!

You just started talking to Jackson?

Yeah, I was talking with the shoeshine man anyway. I never had a problem talking to strangers. That drove my mother crazy. I used to talk to strangers on the bus. This was before they had black bus drivers, so my mother was worried that we would get kicked off.
You could go out there without a problem?

Jackson just walked up to his white boss and said he wanted to show his nephew the trains. No problem. Keep in mind, a loyal Negro worker was trusted, and there were no security threats like today. I went in the Dome car, the *Beavertail* last car, which had 180 degrees of windows and a lounge. Sadly, I was unable to sit in the locomotive. To this day, I have not done that. But now, after talking about trains after all these years, I'm going to visit a railroad museum. Anyway, I kept my eye on the time. I had to make it back to the YMCA before 3pm, just in case my mother came earlier to pick me up.
That's quite an adventure for a kid. How many trips did you make to the train stations?

Only two. But I would often take shorter bus rides until my father saw me getting off one. He had surprised me by picking me up early from the Y. That's something my mother usually did. He didn't say anything right then, but shortly thereafter, my parents took me out of the Y program. Later that summer, to my surprise, he bought a 1959 Cadillac Coupe de Ville, and in August, he drove the family to Los Angeles and San Francisco to sightsee and visit relatives.
You liked to travel around the city and meet people. You and your father were having a great time; how about your mother and sister?

They didn't share our enthusiasm for travel. As time went by more trips were only my father and me. That was good in a way because, as time went on, he became more and more busy with work, and was unable to spend a lot of time with me. So, I'm extremely grateful for those early days we spent together. He strongly influenced my travel and rambling desires, but I doubt if he realized at the time to what extent. He was a train buff, and had been since he was a child. Once when I was a teenager he showed me train schedules he had collected from the 1920s, thirties, and forties, from twenty or more different railroads. He said that studying train schedules, Pullman Porter literature, and Sears and Roebuck catalogs were among the ways he fueled his determination to leave East Texas. He hit the road at age 15.

My mother and sister grew tired of train outings, but in 1956 my father took my sister and me to New York on the New York Central Railroad's second most luxurious train, the *Pacemaker*. There was only one train above it, and that was the magnificent *Twentieth Century Limited*. My father said the only reason we didn't take that train was that it was sold out. They had a wait list for that train because of its luxury and popularity. *The Pacemaker* had been a luxury all-coach train, but at the time of our trip, sleeper coaches had only recently been added in order to boost the train's luxuriousness.

The trip to New York was overnight—sixteen hours. We had a Pullman compartment that could sleep four people. My sister and I had bunks, and my dad had a bed. When the Pullman Porters came and let the beds down, my father would tip them heavy. He felt a camaraderie with them hard working brothers. He knew most of their earnings were from tips. The food was excellent, the ride was smooth, and the train arrived in NYC on time, which was guaranteed by the New York Central Railroad. If the train was late there was some type of compensation. In the case of the *Twentieth Century Limited,* if it arrived late, each passenger received a silver dollar coin for each minute the train was late.

We stayed at the Hotel Theresa in Harlem. The Theresa was where many black celebrities and regular people stayed. It was a four-star hotel for Blacks. In those days, Blacks were not welcomed at the posh hotels in Manhattan, and if they were, the room deposit was greater for Blacks than for Whites. Even Fidel Castro and his entourage stayed at the Theresa when they came to New York for meetings at the United Nations. Nikita Khrushchev, Nehru, and Castro had meetings there. Many of the era's best-known Blacks, including Malcolm X and Josephine Baker lived or stayed in the Theresa, which was sometimes referred to as the Waldorf of Harlem.

My father went to New York to take care of some type of legal business for his older half- brother, Dell. I've never known the nature of the business, but I remember riding around in Dell's 1955 Cadillac Fleetwood that was driven by a white chauffeur. I remember the fine dining with him at the Hotel Theresa where he was well known. In the restaurant, he was recognized by jazz musicians and local business people. Once in the restaurant, he and tenor sax player Paul Gonzales, who played with legendary band leader and composer Duke Ellington, warmly greeted and hugged each other. Dell said, "Hey, how you doing, what's happening, baby, how's Duke?" Paul responded, "Mellow man, Duke's cool... Good to see you, Dell. I'm just in here for a minute. On my way to meet some of the cats right now." Then Dell introduced my father and us children. And one thing Dell did as part of any introduction was to say, "My brother here is a great lawyer in Chicago." Then he would give my father's business card. Dell would promote my dad whenever he could. My dad said that over the years Dell had referred many clients, whose business helped pay many bills.

Sounds like Dell moved around in several circles. What kind of look did Dell have. How did he present himself?

Knowing the right people and moving around the country was his forte. But his secrets of survival outside of gambling remain a mystery. My parents never told me all that he did, but you know, given his times and circumstances, I have some ideas. No doubt he was an accomplished hustler. People can interpret that as they please.

One thing for sure is that he was a sharp dresser. He had suits tailored by Lytton's and Rothschild's and other fine stores in Chicago and elsewhere. His hats were by Stetson, Dobbs, or custom made. His shoes were Allen Edmonds and Florsheim until the quality declined. He was slightly over six feet tall, and thin, with a darker complexion. I guess he weighed around 180 pounds. My mother called him a dandy. He died in Chicago around 1962. I remember my parents saying that he had 30 pairs of shoes and over 50 suits in closet. Most of his expensive clothes were donated to charity. But you know, Dell would be considered extravagant by most standards. But back in those days, a man in a suit could command a certain amount of respect. Black men and women usually dressed nicely, not only out of respect for themselves, but to show the Whites that we are a viable and valuable people. And Dell had it in for white folks, so he dressed so well partially to outdo and embarrass them.

Dell seems like some people you find in Chester Himes' novels

who are really able to navigate through the post-Reconstruction maze with keen survival instincts. Can you please tell us more about Dell?**

Most of what I know is from what I heard my parents say when I was a child. Also, a few recollections from my aunt Viola, who was the youngest in the family, so her recollection are sometimes vague, or what she was told by others. And some stories Dell related while I was in his presence. I remember his rambling on about his life around us kids was discouraged by my parents. My father, and other members of his family, were sometimes reluctant to talk about race-related events that happened back in East Texas that may have affected the lives of Dell and my father.

Do you think they found some memories too disturbing?

Certainly. And that was typical of that generation. People had pain they didn't want to speak about. They both vowed never to return to Texas. And after I got older, whenever I spoke about having to go to Texas for any reason, my father would suddenly shift from his usually calm persona and insist that whatever I had to do in Texas could be done elsewhere. "Stay out of Texas!" he would say emphatically.

Dell used different names: Dell Henderson, Dell Beauchamp, and Emmet Cleaver, among many. The latter is said to be his birth name. Dell was my father's half-brother. Sometimes my father referred to him as "my mother's child."

Let me add something here so that you can picture the lay of the land. My dad's family lived on a tenant farm outside of Rusk, Texas, the same property some of them had lived on during slave times. They raised pigs, cows, other farm animals and grew several types of crops. A story told by most of my father's kin is that Dell got into some Emmett Till type of trouble, and when the Whites came after him, he was ready for them. Everyone agrees that Dell was a tough motherfucker who was not afraid of white people. Two young white men made the mistake of trying take Dell down out in the woods. They seriously got their asses whupped. One of them may have never fully recovered from the beating he received. My father related that one evening just before sunset, Dell came out the nearby pine woods and said that he had to leave quickly. He said some white men had tried to beat him, but he got the best of them, and they were in the woods badly hurt. He told the family not to be surprised if Judge So-and-So came looking for him, as they were his sons. Dell wrapped some clothes in a shirt and rolled it into carrying bundle. Then, along with his dog, a huge long-haired cur named Grendel, walked up a hill on a dirt road that eventually crossed a railroad track. At the top of the hill Dell turned and waved, then disappeared. That was the last time anyone saw him for 30 years, but Grendel returned to the farm a week later. Dell never saw his parents again. This was in 1914. Dell was sixteen years old, my father, eleven. Two days later the judge and his two boys showed up on horseback looking for Dell. They searched the property, found nothing, but the family was routinely harassed until they all moved away.

My father left in 1918 at the age of fifteen. He headed to San Antonio and eventually the Juarez, Mexico area, where, as he put it, he enjoyed new-found freedom and the pleasures that a young man should experience.

Everyone eventually left the farm. When did your dad learn what happened to Dell during thirty-five years?

Dell eventually located Fanny, the eldest sister who was living in Dallas. Fanny provided Dell with family contacts. Dell told my dad he had enlisted in the Army in 1916 and was deployed to France with the 369th infantry, who were also called the Harlem Hellfighters. The Germans were retreating from France in late 1918, and the French, exhausted and badly in need of fighters, asked General Pershing for help. That's how the black infantries got involved in the war, and some wore the uniform of French soldiers. Dell, like many other black soldiers, had life-changing experiences. They were treated as equals, they were celebrated and given prestigious medals for service, valor, and courage; they interacted with Africans, they experienced freedom of movement, and they socialized with whomever they wanted. This was of course most disturbing to the core thinking of racist and repressive white America, including the U.S. government. When the jubilant black soldiers returned home expecting at the very least praise and recognition for their contribution, some were lynched, even in uniform, and others were more marginalized by white America and remained targets of institutionalized racism. Dell found more freedom in Alaska. There, he made a living as a gambler for several years. He said there were so few black people there that Whites never bothered him, and many of them thought of themselves as outcast from the lower forty-eight states. This was years before Alaska became a state.

Did your family travel or vacation together?

Yes, but that was when my sister and I were younger. In the late fifties my father's business started to pick up, and that was rewarding for him because he had been a lawyer since 1932. It was a very difficult in the beginning: The Great Depression, World War Two, and the lack of opportunity in the United States' legal sector. In 1956, the family took its longest train ride, from Chicago to San Francisco, to visit with my father's sister, Viola. We rode the *Challenger* on the Milwaukee Road to Ogden, Utah, then headed into Oakland on the Union Pacific *Domeliner*. I was seven years old and having a blast looking out of the window, playing games with my sister, and enjoying the wonderful custom cooked meals. Not like the Amtrak plasti-meals served today. Railroad companies went to great lengths to provide good food and comfort. And in a way, black travelers had an advantage over Whites: most of the service people were black (cooks, porters, servers, redcaps). They were happy to see other Blacks traveling in a style usually only enjoyed by Whites, many of whom were extremely demanding, and often called most black railroad workers as George, after George Pullman, creator of Pullman railroad sleeper coaches. It was demeaning, and it implied that black workers were owned by their boss and had no real identity. When I was growing up I came to know several men who had been cooks for the railroads. Some of them told me that it was common practice that when an arrogant White would ask to speak to the white chef boss to complain about something, just because they could, they would re-do the order, this time farting on it. And the customer would invariably remark, "This is much better, boy." One retired cook I know told me about how he chafed between his legs because of the heat in the kitchen and would apply ample amounts of Vaseline to soothe the irritation. When somebody sent their meal back to him for no reason, he would drop a dollop of Vaseline from around his balls and ass into the frying pan or mix it in with a sauce or pancakes. And again, the customer expressed approval with the new preparation. Ha-ha! Booty berries in your biscuits and gravy!

Keep it coming.

I recall when I was around three or four my mother wanted to enroll me in nursery school, or daycare as it's now called. Today there stands on the northeast corner of Oakwood Boulevard and Langley Avenue the Northeastern Illinois University Center for Inner City Studies. The building used to be called Abraham Lincoln Center, which housed a public library, auditorium, recreational center, and nursery school on the top floor. My mother wanted to enroll me, but the administrators said I was too big and may hurt the other children. They had never seen a child my size. Of course, my mother was hurt and called my father, extremely upset, to say what had happened. The effect on me was not immediate, but the more I heard my parents speak about it, the more I became aware of my size, which prior to this situation, I had not thought about. I was just enjoying being a child. Oddly, as a teenager about fifteen years after this incident, I saw a concert by the Association for the Advancement of Creative Musicians in the same facility, and five years later, I would be working with AACM members and eventually writing a book about the Art Ensemble of Chicago.

I've seen photos where you are the tallest child in your class. Was your childhood was affected by your size?

Definitely. In a size, diet, and make-up obsessed society, so often those who are outside of the norm are going to be singled out, and sometimes demeaned. The American standard by which people's looks are measured is of course, average looking white people—white, supposedly heterosexual males, and Barbie Doll-looking women. And this brainwashing over centuries affected Blacks to the point of not appreciating their own beauty. And some white people, they've spent millions trying to fit the mold. Also, there's big profit in failure to do so, as I've been told by psychoanalysts friends of mine.

There are the anorexics, the obese, the little people, and of course the so called "beautiful people," who many people want to look like, including the ones who are certified idiots. And then there are those who are made to feel, if they allow it, that because of their size they should put it to some special use. A tall person should play basketball, a big guy should play football, and so on. Taller and bigger people also have an additional pressure of often having to prove themselves. Unusual people, not only in looks, but also intelligence in either extreme, are among the favorite targets of bullies and cowards. I found this to the case throughout my school days. And the same happens today. Actually, it's more tragic with the use of social media. I mean, when I was coming up you never heard about self-harming and such. But the bullies during my time were not necessarily limited to other students. There was institutionalized bullying by the teachers at my school who were nuns and priests. And there were church flunkies, whose entire interaction with nearly all the students centered around tactics of denigration and instilling fear. On top of this, add a child being heavy, slow, short, super smart, etc., combined with racism. The result is what I, and many others, experienced on a day-to-day basis as students at Holy Angels School and at Mt. Carmel High School in Chicago, and without a doubt elsewhere. In terms of students, there have always been bullies in schools and on playgrounds. But once you kick their ass, that shit's over. And I didn't have no problem going to blows with the toughest dudes in school. Kicked their ass like a bad habit.

The nuns and priests were far worse than the kids in school, as they were grown and completely responsible for their actions?

Exactly. And as you know, some type of abuse, denigration, and hypocrisy are key to the insidious Catholic long-term "own your mind, body, soul, children, and money" process. The Jesuits were slave traders and slave owners in Maryland. The Dominicans were the Inquisition thug crew. The Carmelites, Franciscans, and other religious orders have been major players in genocide through political power, association with royalty, and the evil and cruel practice of dispatching militaries and missionaries to create havoc and dissent in cultures thousands of years old, like the indigenous people of Africa, the Americas, and Asia. How many cultures have been exploited, diseased, murdered, and eventually annihilated? Man, think about the Arawak people. Ain't no more. Wiped out! How many have had their women, men, and children raped, maimed, and murdered at the hands of these "messengers of Christ"? I don't want to digress too

much, but I think Jesus Christ was not a Christian. He was probably a good person; that's why his own greedy people fucked him up. Some people talk about being Christ-like? What the fuck does that even mean? Religious orders, in my opinion and experience, tend to be odious sects consisting of perverts, racists, cowards, bullies, mass manipulators, and more evil shit than I can think of now. And they are often complicit in geopolitical atrocities, hiding behind the veil of neutrality, when they are in bed with dictators, Nazis, and repressive governments. Remember, control, power, and cash are the crux.
About Holy Angels, my understanding is that parishioners have insisted on the inclusion of African-American traditions in the services. How was it when you were there?

I don't know what's going on there today from any firsthand experience. I only know what I and others experienced during my time there. Back in the seventies, I think I heard that they started a Black Mass and have included some traditional African-American religious customs in their services and the addition of black priests. The white church hierarchy now allows them to shout "Amen," and maybe wave their hands around. The priests even adorn themselves in Kente cloth and have allowed African influenced music. It's sickening. The same motherfuckers that called you "heathens" will do anything to keep the cash coming. One black priest, George Clements, who adopted children against the wishes of the Cardinal, was at the forefront of the Black Catholic movement. Adopting was important to demonstrate the need for Blacks to look out for each other in general. The Cardinal finally backed off Clements. Strangely though, Clements went from being regularly in the news to almost never mentioned. Nothing for years. I think he was semi-exiled– put out to pasture.

Anyway, if they wanted to keep black people as members, especially during the Civil Rights movement and later, adjustments to their practices and attitude would be essential. But if those adjustments were made, it was more about the bottom line than a sudden love and respect for all things Black. As far as black priests are concerned, I think the whole Roman Catholic system is a gigantic con game that began with Constantine and will continue, until, like all things, time takes it away. Black priests are part of the con, or maybe some of them are duped, or just plain stupid. Many black Catholics dream of the day that a Black may become Pope. If that happens, that would be one of the darkest moments in the history of Africa's progeny.

The Holy Angels School I knew was a dark and evil place. The buildings were, and still are, austere in appearance. We students called the main building a prison. Teachers were white except for two African American nuns with questionable sanity. All the students were black except for the Michalowski twins. There were around one thousand students. Each classroom had around fifty or sixty students and one teacher. No teacher's aides or helpers. Each grade had two classrooms. So, that's nine by one hundred twenty or so. Yeah, around a thousand black children under the yoke of extreme racism enforced by a corps of violent, ignorant, inept, and culturally deprived teaching-nuns who operated under the governance of the School Sisters of Saint Francis, headquartered in Milwaukee, Wisconsin. I don't know what evil, chilling fluid ran through the veins of these women; it's hard to believe that it was human blood. There was also a corps of trained boot-licking lackeys who, upon being commanded to do so, would beat the shit out of any kid that they were ordered to. The lead lackey was a 350-pound brute, Anderson Nelson. Not only would he beat any child he was ordered to, he would also beat his own children if asked. He was such a pathetic, groveling son-of-a-bitch that my father nicknamed "The Holy Angels Man." They owned him.

Did you have any confrontations with the Holy Angels Man?

I did. I mean this ignorant motherfucker was all the way off the chain. Back in 1960, I must have been in fifth grade. John Kennedy and Richard Nixon were running for president. Kennedy was a Catholic, so naturally most Catholics were for him. He was also a Democrat. Now, my father was for Nixon. Why? Because the southern democratic politicians were at the forefront of Jim Crow, lynching, the KKK, and white supremacy. You know, Dixiecrats. It was President Dwight Eisenhower who sent federal troops to Little Rock to forcefully allow black children to attend schools. Eisenhower and Nixon were Republicans. Abe Lincoln was Republican. Understandably, my father didn't trust the Democrat Party. One day,

I decided to wear a Richard Nixon-Henry Cabot Lodge campaign button to school. I was 11 or so; I wasn't thinking about much of anything politically. I wore it because my father had it around the house, and he had been talking about the Republicans, the Presidency, and Little Rock. I didn't put the button on until I got to school because had he seen it, he probably would not have allowed me to wear it.

I'm visualizing. Here you are in a Catholic thicket walking around with a Nixon-Lodge button. Okay Beau, what happened?

Wearing that button was a big mistake. The Holy Angels Man was walking out of the cafeteria building as my class was walking in for lunch. When he saw that button on my coat, he grabbed me by the collar of my coat and punched me in the stomach until I was breathless. All the time he was ranting about Kennedy being Catholic. He was furious...enraged. Then he caught himself and just walked away. The other kids just keep going into the lunch room. I told a nun what happened; I don't think anything happened to him. I told my parents. I don't know if they believed me or not. I know my father had the potential for great anger, and I think he wanted to avoid a confrontation. I vowed to kick the Holy Angels Man's ass one day, somehow, but that never happened.

You know these stories of cruelty and all types of abuse are quite common. No one's pain can be rectified by apologies or the courts. Prevention is key. The fear factor must be reversed. If you bother our children, we gonna fuck you up. That means prison and payments. And it could mean a personal touch as well. If a priest, nun, or any of them touch my children or family...big trouble for them.

I'm with you LaBosse. Same here.

All right. If you please, more.

I attended kindergarten at Holy Angels in 1955, then in 1956 my family moved to the West Side of Chicago to 1111 South Independence Boulevard, which was near a church called Sainte-Finbarr at 14thStreet and Harding Avenue where I attended first grade. My time there was rather uneventful, but the priests had the practice of dropping by the houses of stay-at-home mothers and other women who were at home alone, unannounced. I remember my parents speaking about this, as one of the priests had dropped by to see my mother unannounced, expecting to be cordially received. No way. Controlling every aspect of your life is the goal of indoctrination. It happens across the board in churches, some meditation societies, ashrams, sobriety cults, etc. The bottom line *is* the bottom line– to get what you got: money, property, children, wife, husband, your very soul– all in the name of bringing you closer to the creator, or as some claim, closer to yourself. But they omit the fact that if you give them all you got, you don't have a self anymore. Well, this priest said he just wanted to chat about spiritual matters and wanted get to know my mother and family situation better. What a pile of bull. Over the years his numerous affairs were exposed. For some reason, a few years later, the church and school were demolished.

I went back to Holy Angels School from second through eighth grade, even though we continued to live on the West Side until spring of 1963. The commute was terrible, having to take several buses, but in the spring of 1958 my father bought his first car, a two-tone blue, two-door Ford Custom 300, then the trip was easier to bear. Holy Angels was a rough ride for seven years, fraught with violent, racist teachers, child labor, and complete disrespect for the culture and history of black people.

You said child labor?

Oh, yeah. From about fourth grade on, the boys were forced to unload a semi and carry twenty-five and fifty-pound sacks of potatoes and rice up several flights of steps. We also carried cases of giant cans of other food. I mean, some of the children were exhausted and complaining of asthma and other conditions, and I had back pain.

Did anyone else try to help you?

Absolutely not. Priests, nuns, and flunkies just stood by and gave orders. Occasionally, the Holy Angels Man would grab a sack and sling it over his shoulder, to show us how it's to be done. And if a child was exhausted or became ill, there was no nurse. Can you imagine, a school with a thousand students and no school nurse?

This school seems in many ways more severe than a reform school for delinquents and criminals.

Oh, it was, with the beatings, humiliation, degradation, and total lack of anything pleasant. The playgrounds were cobblestone and gravel. There was nothing for children to play on, not even swings or a slide. In fact, Holy Angels was a microcosm of the idea that black people are inherently bad and thugs not deserving anything pleasant. That we are savages rescued from Africa and should be grateful. That we are defiant of White established order—or really, disorder, when you look at their history.

What did you do during recess?

We usually chased each other around. Some girls would try to skip rope and play double-dutch, but that wasn't so easy on gravel. If someone was injured from a fall, which happened nearly every day, a nun would place a band-aid. I got hit in the head with a brick by a troubled boy, Ron White, and I definitely needed stitches. They should have called an ambulance, but I got gauze and tape. I still have that scar in my left eyebrow.

Tell me more.

I recall in sixth grade asking a nun about African languages. Her response was that Africans didn't have any specific languages, they just grunted, pointed, and yelled meaningless syllables at each other to make a point. She emphasized that being naked savages, they had not evolved enough to have a definable language, but missionaries were making progress educating them and creating a written language. I once got smacked for calling a buddy "Negro," as black people often do in jest. Imagine, the wench that smacked me was regularly calling us children savages, heathens, darkies, picaninnies, filthy, stinking, Hottentots, and much more. They called us all these names, but the nuns were the stinkiest people I have ever been around. Lord only knows what was going on underneath those habits they wore. I mean, when some of them walked past, I could smell farts, stinking pussy, armpits, and everything else creeping from under there. And some were extremely ugly, *bruta*; one nun, Genevieve, had a five o'clock shadow by noon, along with her stinking ass.

Even though they used the word Hottentot as a derogatory term, I must point out here they were among the many African tribes who resisted colonization, and their proper name is *Khoikhoi*, which translates to "People People" or "Real People." The European *unsettlers* couldn't pronounce it, or most likely didn't care about what

they called themselves. The Germans massacred them by the thousands in the early 1900s. Tell me, who are the real savages?
I hear you, Brother.

What I'm saying now are things that happened to me or that I witnessed. Starting in second grade I was singled out to be made an example of. The first day of the school year, while standing in the lunch line holding my tray, I was humming a song to myself, a melody from an Ajax cleanser TV commercial. It went something like "Ajax, baboom baboom, boom-boom." I mean, it was barely audible. Then, walking along the lunch line as though looking beyond me came a nun named Sister Crateria. She approached on my right. She then turned slightly to her left while saying, "Keep quiet!" Then she spun around to her right and attacked with a full knuckled, backhand closed fist across my face. I fell back, dropping my lunch tray and food. "Pick it up," she demanded. I just cried and cried. There is no way in the world I was going to pick it up. One of the flunkies came and cleaned it up. So, here is a case of being singled out for a couple of reasons: I was the tallest kid and she needed to embarrass me in front of the other children just to demoralize, and she needed to assert her authority. Being a bully, a coward, and ugly, she figured by decking the biggest child, the other children were less likely to cause problems. I was tall for my age, but still within the range of a child in my age group, seven years old. Here is a grown person, thirty-five or forty years old, knocking the shit out of a second grader. Now, the nuns knew my parents were educated, and that may have also been part of Crateria's motivation. The nuns and priests resented educated Blacks, or anyone that represented possible resistance to their program. They preferred the uneducated and surrounded themselves with groveling, obedient lackeys, who cheerfully, and often fearfully, did whatever they were told. This brute that attacked me was a dense kitchen hag; her "calling" was cooking for black children and scrubbing floors, pots, and pans. Over the months that followed, her resentment towards me continued to grow. I mean, among her own people, she was living beneath the bottom rung. She resented Blacks, this wedding ring wearing, self-proclaimed, bride of Jesus.

Another thing—the children, including me, were often sick in the stomach. There was frequent diarrhea and vomiting. The food was absolutely sickening in taste and smell, and I never saw a priest or nun eating it. But they did entertain guests at the convent and rectory, and I'm sure the slop we kids ate wasn't on their menu.

This must have been traumatic for you. I'm trying to imagine your pain, and in a way, your innocence and confidence in adults being crushed. As a child, one needs to feel nurtured and loved while being taught valuable lessons by sensible adults. What did your parents think of this incident?

I told my mother, but she thought I was exaggerating. Not only in this instance, but others through the years. My parents thought that I embellished my reports about school, but years later they would come to understand just what was going on. Unfortunately, because of their upbringing, even though they had horrible experiences growing up in the southern United States, they wanted to believe that they were accepted by the Catholic Church, and that the nuns and priests were essentially good people who would not harm children. So for a time, indoctrination had a grip on my entire family. But my parents eventually had a rude awakening when my sister went away at Alverno College in West Allis, Wisconsin. She had to defend herself against sexual assault by nuns. As for nurturing, or any kind or positive interaction with children, the nuns possessed neither the knowledge, interest, or experience. Remember, to them we were darkies and heathens, and they the brides of Jesus. How could they be wrong? Such fucking ignorance!

After Holy Angels, you attended Mt. Carmel High School. What was that like?

I'll tell you about a thing that happened in high school that had a positive result, and that was not the intention of the priests or school administration. Mt. Carmel High School had a disciplinarian, a violent oaf by the name of Jordon Rooney. My confrontations with Rooney eventually led to my dismissal from school.

There were only a handful of Blacks in the school, and they were there primarily to participate in sports. When I took the entrance exam, which I didn't want to take, I randomly filled in the dots in the multiple-choice questions, hoping to eliminate or lessen the possibility of being accepted. The various tests were to last five hours; I was finished and was out of there in two. I did not want to go to an all-boys school, and I didn't want to go to a school with mostly hostile white boys. I didn't want to go to a Catholic school. I wanted to go to a co-ed, culturally diverse, and academically challenging school. Within a week after the tests, I got a letter of acceptance and a call from the football coach inviting me to try out for the team. Well, I didn't make the team, primarily because I didn't give a fuck about football or helping Mt. Carmel win anything. I did not want to be used. Also, I couldn't stand the coach who was constantly barking like a ravenous dog and calling the tryouts pansies and sissies, along with remarks about those with darker complexions. But even back then I was hep to the inadequacies in these men that cause such behavior, and really, the sissies are the ones calling other folks sissies. Think about that coach out at Penn State. Of course, I'm not saying they all are. But you know, those hazing practices in soccer and other sports…?

The football coaches and priests could not believe that I had no interest in playing football. What else was a big black kid supposed to do in life other than play sports, serve white people, shine shoes or dig ditches? Maybe retire after football with what's left of his brain from taking too many concussions, get a job promoting a car dealership, or maybe hit the big time and get to play a slave in a movie. Back then pro athletes didn't make nearly the kind of money that they make today, and they had very few benefits or options upon retirement. I so much disliked the whole physical fitness program at this school because of the screaming and ethnic slurs that I devised a way not to participate in anything at all after what I'm about to tell you.

I reluctantly joined the wrestling team in my freshmen year and lost nearly every match. Then the unthinkable happened: one day I was in gym for intramural wrestling, and I had forgotten my gym t-shirt at home, so I had on an Italian knit shirt that I kept in my locker to change into as soon as I was away from the school. Well, the football coach who liked to bark out, "sissy" and "pansy" was also the wrestling coach and gym instructor. A real *Mr. Fitness*. On this particular day, the coach called me to the mat to wrestle. He shouted out, "Who wants to wrestle Beauchamp?" It was like a gladiator arena. The white boys wanted blood. They called for Mike

Vaughn, a senior who was a defensive tackle on the football team. Known for his toughness, and ripping apart opponents, the white boys thought he'd surely wipe the mat with me. "Ready, wrestle," commanded the coach. Vaughn charged, growling and nearly foaming at the mouth. He fucked up. He ripped my Italian knit shirt that I had worked hard to buy. Hell no! Big mistake. I lifted his ass off the ground, threw him down hard on the mat, put him in a cradle hold, locked my hands, and tried to break his neck. They had to pull me off him. Now, some people can experience something and not believe what they've experienced. That was the case here. The white boys starting shouting, "Again, again." Vaughn roars forward. This time I pinned him with a traditional hold in about twenty seconds, squeezed his neck as hard as I possibly could. That was the end of Mike's BMOC days. He had been defeated by a freshman, a big black pansy, the guy who didn't want to play football. For a while I enjoyed the accolades from most of the black students, and a few of the white ones too, especially those that had been bullied by Vaughn and his crew, the coaches, and priests. But whipping Vaughn's ass did not sit well with Rooney, who was looking for any reason to mess with me after that.

The football hero and BMOC got his ass kicked by a freshman. Now you've got white boys, coaches, and priests riled-up, and pissed off. What were the repercussions?

Some of them motherfuckers were upset for a while, especially Rooney. The coaches quickly converted my victory into some type of motivational tool, and the white boys eventually calmed down. But Jordan, that bullying motherfucker, as I said, was out for blood.

Jordan's dislike for you just kept on growing?

Not just dislike, out-and-out hatred. I could feel it. See it in his eyes. Like I said, I'd had it with all of fitness, sports attitude, "use-a-Negro" attitude at Mt. Carmel. I had proven myself as a wrestler; now it was time for me to spend that PE and sports time the way I wanted. In my sophomore year, I claimed an allergy to the chlorine in the shower water and had my doctor write a note stating that. This got me a free period which I usually spent in the library reading selections I had brought with me from home. One day I was reading James Baldwin's *Another Country*. Rooney, who spent most of time administering beatings with a huge belt or a tennis shoe to bare-assed boys, or gazing at boys in the shower, crept up behind me and snatched my book from me. I was wondering why he was in the library. I later learned that he had been summoned by the spineless librarian who chose not to confront me personally about what I was reading. Rooney ranted, "How dare you bring this black filth to this school. Don't you know that we don't tolerate this kind of smut?"

He confiscated my book, my property, and summarily sentenced me to a week of detention. That meant coming to school an hour earlier than usual and doing some type of labor about the school grounds. I protested. I told him that he had no right to take my property, pass judgment, and mete out punishment simply because he didn't like who I was reading. I did not show up for dentition. Fuck that. Well, I paid the price for that. The following day, Jordan blindsided me during lunch in the cafeteria. It was exactly what some of these ignorant motherfuckers are doing today with the "knockout" game: surprise your victim with a punch intended to knock them out. I wasn't knocked out, but knocked down. A few minutes later, outside of the lunchroom, Jordan attacked, knocking me down again, but this time with a few kicks to the ribs along with a few choice words that centered on his authority and denigrated my size, complexion, and culture. Culture is an important word here. Most of the black students wanted to fit in so they left their culture at home. They came to school acting out a role to please the Whites. I didn't. No matter what the black students did, they were on the bottom tier of a hierarchy that went like this: at the top were the Irish, who were also key administrators and majority of students, next the Poles, the Italians, followed by other Caucasians such as Greeks or white Hispanics, and, lastly, the Blacks. Interestingly, I heard my first ethnic slurs at Mt. Carmel, as Euro-tribalism was a deep part of the White's culture. They called each other Degos, Wops, Polacks, and anything else that came to mind. And they had occasional fist fights defending their origins.

But the Blacks who excelled in sports circumvented the pecking order a bit because of their usefulness. Anyway, I got myself together and got up from the ground. My sports coat was ripped, my ribs were bruised... I had been totally humiliated. I vowed revenge.

The next day, I put on my best suit, shined my shoes, etcetera—I was impeccable. This was my killing attire. I went to Rooney's office with the intention of taking him out, either by stabbing or gunshot. I had everything I needed in my book satchel. His office was busy, lots of coming and going. There was a secretary for several administrators who shared the same general area. She said I'd have to wait a bit. Jordan peeped out of his office, with a smirk on his face, and told me he'd be with me soon. He was busy cutting a boy's hair who had been warned that his hair was too long. This ignorant motherfucker thought I was there to apologize. I was there to fuck him up good. Fortunately for both of us, he was busy. While he was cutting hair, I had time to think. I thought about my family and how my parents had survived this same kind of bullshit on a much larger scale and had outsmarted every ignorant, racist sumbitch that had tried to block their way. And I thought, there is no way I'm going to walk away from my actions. I could totally wipe him out, as well as my future, in the next few minutes. I told the secretary I had to go to the restroom. I just left the school, walked down to 63rd street, found my man Smitty in the poolroom, and gave him back the nickel-plated .38 I had borrowed, and dumped the knife. That was the first and last time I've possessed a firearm.

Okay. Your property was stolen, you were beaten, and you were marginalized by these men who allege that they are specifically servants of the Blessed Virgin, mother of Jesus.

That whole concept is perplexing, eerie. But let's assume that their concept is real and good. Then what do these people I'm talking with have to do with anything that is good? "Not nothing!" as my friend Pinetop Perkins used to say. And they know it. And it's amusing to watch the Catholic Church try to resell itself with public relations chicanery. With the new pope, Francis, they are just re-lubing the same old machinery with a slightly different twist. I just read that the Vatican has endorsed the idea of a Palestinian State. On the surface, that seems like a good move, but I think the Palestinians should keep a sharp eye on the Pope. The Catholic Church always has the *bottom line* as its number one priority.

Other thoughts on Mt. Carmel?

I want to put a lot of the blame for my mistreatment, and that of others, squarely where it belongs, and that is on the shoulders, if he has any, of Thaddeus J. O'Brien, O. C., who was the principal of the school. O. C. stands for "Order of Carmel," but really, it's "Order of Cowards." Now think about this. You have a child, fourteen, fifteen years old being severely beaten, his property stolen, and he is verbally abused. There is no contact with parents, there is no discussion after the fact to try to find a solution. There is absolutely no communication regarding what happened. It's as if they are so right in what they do– why should anything be discussed? And I'm sure you know that's the same position taken with handling priest pederasts, pedophiles, rapists, and other offenders. It's not until the motherfuckers are cornered that they offer any kind of comment or strained apology for PR reasons. Thaddeus J. O'Brien permitted this abuse, and he should be held accountable. And one day that may happen. Hopefully, the law will eventually confront all of the Catholic Church's abuses besides the well-known sexual ones. The organization SNAP has been successful in bringing some low-life Catholic clergy to justice. I wish them continued success.

Can you think of anything positive about your Catholic experience?

Well, because of who I am as a person, I naturally resisted what I instinctively felt was designed to repress rather than uplift, to keep people poor and submissive, rather than provide a framework for advancement. It didn't take me long to start questioning what I was being taught. The godliness of nuns and priest was becoming increasingly unbelievable. The life of Christ as they told it, and the way they behaved, were completely opposite. I think if there is such an entity or maybe energy that's an Antichrist, it has its birthplace, history, and home in that shit-hole of massive wealth and hypocrisy the Vatican. So, the positive thing that happened was my awakening, albeit gradual, and often painful. Physically painful because they beat the shit out of me, and mentally because I spent so many years immersed in it as a child. There is gratification when one finally emerges from the dark tunnels of hate, lies, racism, control, hypocrisy, and other evils into the light of the living!

After Mt. Carmel, was that it for you and the Catholic Church?

Yeah, pretty much. But a couple of things happened that finally sealed it for me. I was kicked out after my sophomore year. My parents wanted to quickly enroll me into another school. There was a private school called Harvard-Saint George, located in Chicago's Kenwood neighborhood. It was well respected and prestigious. I met all the requirements to attend; however, Mt. Carmel added a note to my transcripts saying that I had brought pornographic books to school, referring to the James Baldwin novel I was reading in the library. I found out later that Mt. Carmel did not specifically mention Baldwin in the transcripts, only the word "pornography." Had they mentioned Baldwin, I think things would have played out differently. You see the nature of them evil Carmelite motherfuckers!

I was not accepted at Harvard-Saint George because my moral character was questionable. So, I attended Hyde Park High School night classes. Interestingly, the great Bluesman Howlin' Wolf was in my geometry class, though he rarely attended because of his hectic schedule.

Other things that happened?

I always thought that the sacraments were weird, but confession was the weirdest. Going to confession is one the most despicable inventions of the Catholic Church. How wicked, manipulative, sexist, and fucking arrogant to have a person go and confess to some asshole, who depending on what you say, may be in the confessional masturbating, or use what you've said to blackmail, or "white male" you. How goddamn gullible and afraid are people to believe that this person in a booth has the power to forgive, or not forgive, and to mete out punishments. Believe me, that's some Dark Ages bullshit. That's as sinister as inquisitions and witch burnings.

One day I decided to go to confession at Old Saint Mary's Church located on the corner of Wabash and Van Buren in downtown Chicago, a nearly all-white congregation operated by the Paulist Fathers. But not one confession, but two, in order to see how the penance would differ. I decided to confess the same fictional sins in two different confessionals. Here's how it went: I said I'm a homosexual, I had stolen a golden chalice from a church, and that I was a heroin addict who occasionally turned tricks to support my habit. The first confessor wanted details about turning tricks. I said

everything I could think of. He cleared his throat and said, "Say a Rosary. Go and sin no more." Then I went to another confessional and told that priest the same sins. He listened, then said, "You are banished from the Holy Catholic Church. You are excommunicated and condemned to Hell." I said, "You mean there's nothing I can do?" He said, "No, nothing." "Not even if I completely reform?" "Nothing." I said, "Thank you, asshole," and left. I've not been to a Catholic ceremony of any sort since that day fifty years ago. Hooray!
One last question on this. Why were you Catholic?

I'm glad you asked because the answer gives me the opportunity to speak about my mother and her family. My mother, Betty Smith, was number ten of fourteen children. She was born into a farming family in 1906 near Henderson, Kentucky. In her family were several preachers, and her father was a deacon in the Missionary Baptist Church. Back in those days the MB church was quasi-sanctified, lots of animation, speaking in tongues, and trances. One of my cousins, Reverend O.B. Smith, now pastors a church in Tuscumbia, Alabama.

My mother came from Black, African-rooted worship. The Catholic mutterings in Latin, the liturgy, and the Euro-centric confining and rigid style of worship were completely foreign to her—and boring. When she and my father moved to Chicago in 1940, a friend introduced them to Saint Thomas, a Black Episcopal congregation. It was a kind of meeting place for Great Migration new arrivals– a place to get acclimated to Chicago life. My mother loved it because the church had a thriving social atmosphere. Lots of fashion shows, teas, trips, etcetera, but it still lacked the kind of excitement she was used to. My godparents and my sisters came from that church. I remember being around three or four years old having a good time playing in Saint Thomas' playroom. When my sister—who was born in 1945— became school-aged, my parents thought she would get a better education in a Catholic school. Fact is, other private schools were not affordable. For some reason, and I'm not sure why, when my sister was in second grade, they transferred her from Saint Elizabeth to Holy Angels. Unfortunately, my fate was sealed by this move as well. Holy Angels insisted that if your child went to the school, the whole family had to attend religious instruction class and convert. That's how we became Catholic. My mother never liked it, but eventually she tried to fit in, much to her and my sister's and my detriment. My father pretended, but at the end of the day, he didn't give a shit about the whole Catholic program.

In closing this section, it's necessary for me to affirm my belief that there are good people in every religion. Organized religion is not my thing, but I think it's important for people whose thing it is not to live in fear, and not to protect those who are known to have caused great harm to others.

That's a wrap?
Boom! That's a wrap!

Ritz Carlton
DECA Bar and Café
Chicago, Illinois
29 December, 2013

Back in Germany, we left off with your ex-communication from the Catholic Church and your family's association with a Black Episcopal Church. Anything to add about the Catholic experience?

Nah, fuck 'em. You want another coffee?

How about the Episcopal Church?

From my perspective as a child, the activities were fun. And my parents enjoyed making new acquaintances. The control factor was not there as it was in the Catholic Church, but a study of the Episcopalian history reveals, in my opinion, many doctrines and practices just as bizarre as those in the Roman Catholic Church.

Shall we move on then?

Let's roll. Wait a moment. Today is my mother's birthday. She was born in 1906. Happy Birthday Mama!

Allright. Happy Birthday, dear Ancestor!

Now, we can continue.

You're no longer in regular school. You're going to night school. How are you spending your time?

I had two scenes outside of the home front. There was my neighborhood scene in the South Shore area on the South Side of Chicago between 67th and 75th streets, Lake Michigan, and Jeffery Avenue, and there was the Hyde Park scene where the University of Chicago is located. These scenes had very different vibes but were also similar in some ways, especially with regards to the Blues and reefer. The neighborhood scene was strictly black, from city-born people, to folks from the Great Migration generations, whereas Hyde Park was a more multicultural environment because of the university.

My activities in my neighborhood consisted of playing lots of basketball, shooting pool, drinking cheap wine and whiskey, smoking and dealing reefer, hanging out with older street hustlers, pimps, whores, numbers runners, pool sharks, and card sharks. And I spent a lot of time trying to talk girls and woman into giving me some pussy. I had no luck, not until I was seventeen. Before that it was beg, beg, beg.

There were people in my neighborhood with names that some in cases reflected their *raison d'être*: Chicken Shack Ron, Slick Head Ron, Bubbles, Jelly Head, Country James, Terrible T, Upper Cut Willis, Cincinnati Al Jordan, Diamond Jim McClain, Plug, Turd, Nickel Plate Slim, Flat Cap Reggie, Snaggletooth Bonnie, Mole Nose Etta, Little Eared Jesse, and Jibbs, who got his name because his bottom lip was hanging down from being shot in the mouth with a .22 caliber pistol by Old Man Collins, owner of the Vogue Lounge on 71st and East End. Jibbs was so mean, he spat the bullet out of his mouth and walked to Jackson Park Hospital at 75th and Stony Island, damn near a mile away.

Anyway, I had reached my adult height by the time I was fourteen. I could buy liquor and get into the nightclubs and lounges without a problem. I hustled pool and worked at the Jewel grocery store on the corner of 71st and Clyde Avenue, so I put a nice wardrobe together. With my *front* together, and a little cash in my pocket, I would hit the South Side clubs looking to party and for ladies. My buddy, Greece, and I would hit the Peps night club on 63rd and Cottage, then stroll east underneath the rumbling "El" Jackson Park line, passing clubs, liquors stores, White's Pool Hall, and maybe end up at The Place at 63rd and Saint Lawrence, where there was always a good blues band. I saw Howlin' Wolf in there many a night. Sometimes we would take it further south to the Bucket of Blood or Fran's Lounge out on Halsted Street, which were known for fine ladies. Another fun thing to do was to leave 63rd and South Park in a jitney cab and ride down to 47th street. Down there was the Regal Theater that had movies and stage shows. You could see a James Bond movie, then see James Brown and the Fabulous Flames on stage. I caught many acts at the Regal. I'm talking Ray Charles, the Marvelettes, B.B. King. Sam and Dave. Always top-notch entertainment. And as a plus, my father's office was located flush upside the Regal in the South Center Building at 417 East 47th Street, right on the corner of South Park Way. Closing out the night meant maybe stopping by the Palm Tavern or the 708 Club on 47th Street, then heading out to the Castle Club or the Vogue Lounge back in the hood at 71st and East

End, or maybe just going home, too drunk to go any further. The South Side was poppin,' baby.

After I got older and had access to a car, we got wild. You know, all the car stuff with girls while listening to WVON DJ's like, Butterball, Lucky Cordell, and Herb Kent "The Cool Gent," playing the latest jams, and Pervis Spann's late-night blues show.

And there were serious house parties that we sometimes called sets, waistline parties, rent parties. Hard Gouster and Ivy League parties. In the nightclubs, police would sometimes be undercover trying to catch people doing what they called "Nasty Dances" like Rufus Thomas' *The Dog* and The Olympics' *The Philly Dog*. Think about it: ignorant, corrupt police trying to exercise moral authority, then take your money and let you continue. If they caught a couple doing *The Dog*, they'd threaten to arrest them for public lewdness unless they paid them off.

How did the Dog go?

Well, it was a precursor to twerking, but with a partner. The girl would twerk on her partner's johnson, usually making it visibly erect. The music was bassy and provocative, and the words instructional: "Do the Dog!"

Was police corruption a part of everyday life?

Yeah, that's one thing I learned growing up in Chicago: keep twenty dollars or so on you because the police are always looking to shakedown somebody. The black police? The only serving and protecting they did was of themselves. They hated themselves, and therefore hated us. I don't think they were allowed to harass white people, or even give them a traffic ticket, or look them in the eye. But when it came to dealing with Blacks, they were devastating.

If they had connections, they could get on the police force illegally like the Whites. I knew guys who were janitors one day, a police the next. They just paid off the right people in the police department. No training, nothing. They got a squad car, some guns, and a badge. Of course, they started shaking people down, yep, made lots of money. In fact, a few years ago there was a badges and DMV investigation. The Feds found police and deputy sheriffs with badges who got salaries because they went out and got votes for some politicians, or did some *favors*. They were flunkies for sleazy Precinct

Captains who are flunkies themselves, some of the most dishonorable characters one can encounter. Their best use was trying to fix usually undeserved traffic and parking tickets. At one point you could buy a driver's license. When I took my road test at sixteen years old, I clipped a twenty onto my DMV paperwork, put it all in the glove box. When the examiner got in my car and asked for the paperwork, I told him to look in the glove box. He took everything and told me to drive through the course and don't stop. He signed off on the paperwork, and I've been driving since then, fifty years.

You know, our readers should internet search "Chicago Greylord Investigation" to get a real sense of the depth of corruption in the city and its courts.

You're how old?

I was sixteen and seventeen. These were two very important years because I got a good sense of how my life was to be, and I began to explore and understand my temperament and priorities. I saw a lot of people doing things I knew I wanted nothing to do with—mostly getting involved with or dragged into some very potentially dangerous situations, like dope deals, fixing sports, or trying to own women. I began to learn the value of freedom early in life—not *only* for me, but everyone else as well.

What was happening on the Hyde Park scene?

That was a whole other bag. My Hyde Park friends were mostly studious with their sights set on college and advanced degrees. The black people I knew thought of themselves as middle class. Most of their parents were professionals: doctors, lawyers, college professors, architects, while most of my neighborhood friends came from agrarian families who had migrated north and become blue collar workers at the steel mills, factories, and stockyards. I had two good friends in Hyde Park, Rani Turner, and Gus Arnold. Both came from families that excelled academically and in the arts. Rani's mother was a school teacher, and his father is still considered the most preeminent linguistic scholars of all time, Dr. Lorenzo Dow Turner, who I mentioned earlier on while speaking about Dhet-DehDeh, and Din-DaDur in a dream. He is often referred to as the Father of Gullah Studies. In the dream, I was on my way to the Turner home when I saw the ass and the monkey wrench.

Gus's family excelled in the arts. He had fifteen brothers and sisters, and their paths of excellence varied greatly, from producing scholarly works to the Blues. Two of his brothers, Billy Boy and Jerome, excelled as blues artists. Billy Boy, who gave me harmonica lessons, gained fame internationally as a songwriter, while his brother, Jerome, a bassist, played with Howlin' Wolf, Paul Butterfield, and others. Update: In 2015, Jerome Arnold was inducted into the Rock and Roll Hall of Fame, along with the original members of the Paul Butterfield Blues Band.

Gus, Rani, and I did lots of planning for our futures. We dreamed together– some real crazy and some not so crazy teenage dreams. At one point, we wanted to be university professors, screwing young women on campus. Then there was the certainty that one if not all of us would win a Nobel Prize for Literature. We aspired to be great writers. This dream was fueled in part by a kind of mentor by the name of Larry Mason. Mason, as we called him, had been a teacher of Gus and Rani at Hyde Park High School, which in former days had been known for academic excellence and cultural diversity, years before such a thing was popular or even acceptable in traditionally segregated Chicago.

Mason's appearance was unique. Ethnically he was of mix of Roma from Hungary and English. He stood about 5-feet, 6-inches tall and weighed about three hundred-fifty pounds. When sitting, he resembled a Buddha statue.

Mason would invite us to his house at 54th and Hyde Park Boulevard, where he and his girlfriend, Beverly, maintained a kind of Parisian, 1930s to fifties-style salon on the weekends. Present at any given time? An assortment of writers, poets, painters, actors, physicists, mathematicians, and chess masters, like Mason. Some were just beginning; others had made great strides in their field. Then there was Gus, Rani, and me, young men invited over to experience the conversation and atmosphere. Our parents were extremely concerned about Mason. My parents were more worried about me going to his house than they were about me running the streets with my neighborhood buddies. The question our parents had was, "Why is this grown man having teenagers come to his home?" They imagined the worst possible goings on: alcohol, drugs, sex orgies, homosexuality, communists. Rani's mother, Lois, became our parents' designated Inspector Clouseau. Early one summer evening there came a loud knock at the front door of the bungalow, which had been divided into several independent residencies. It was in those days called a rooming house, or kitchenettes. Mason's space was huge and located on the first floor with a balcony. The main room, that served all purposes except restroom and kitchen, was around 500 square feet. It was well appointed with a refectory table, comfortable chairs, two sofas, coffee table, stereo, book shelves, liquor cabinet, Persian rugs, exotic lamps, plants, a Remington electric typewriter, and numerous sculptures and other works of art.

There was another bang at the door, then Mrs. Turner noticed a row of doorbells and rang Mason's. It was a friend of Mason's, a gangly, hippyish physicist named Phil Podoner who answered. "I'm looking for my son, Rani Turner. Is he here?" she demanded with an authoritative voice that quivered with nervousness. It was the same authoritative quivering that some aging school teachers and matrons develop from years of screaming at people who usually don't scream back at them. Phil invited Mrs. Turner in. Since Gus, Rani, and I heard her voice, we quickly, and mentally, prepared ourselves for whatever may happen. She entered the room, paused and did a 360-scan of the room. Gus and I greeted her politely. Rani: "Hello Mother." She did not respond. Mason raised himself upright on the sofa where he had been napping and grunted, "Uh hello, I'm Larry Mason." She looked at Larry while sniffing loudly. There was incense burning. Finally, she demanded, "What's that smell?" Before we could answer, "I said, what's that smell?" she shouted. Altogether, but not in unison, we answered. "That's...It's...Uh, incense." Then Larry reiterated with obvious irritation, "Incense Madam, only incense. Not incest, not incensed, as you seem to be. It's incense!"

"What's that noise?" she demanded. I answered that it was John Coltrane, a Jazzman, playing tenor saxophone. She nodded and then gave Rani a piercing glare. She told him to start walking home, which was about a mile away. Gus and I decided to leave as well. So, standing in the middle of the room, looking three times her age because she dressed so homely, wearing old lady lace-up shoes, hair in a bun, no make-up, dowdy and tasteless, stood my friend's mother, addressing Mason: "I'm here to find out exactly what's going on here with you and these boys." And as we were about to leave we heard Larry, now upright and Buddha-like say, "What's going on is what you see, smell, and hear, nothing more. Look around: chessboard, books, music, art, tea, and coffee." Larry continued, "I am a teacher, and these visits from time-to-time are another learning experience. A chance to delve deeper into art and literature, nothing more. But if you want, I will no longer invite them over." By this time we were just about out of the door. Then Mrs. Turner told us to wait. She didn't say a word to Mason, she just turned and left with us.

What was said as y'all walked down the street?

Gus and I were cracking up inside, but were trying to respect our friend's mother. Rani was clearly embarrassed. I told Mrs. Turner that Mason always insisted that when we did visit, we leave no later than around nine in the evening. I tried to assure her that if anything weird was going in his house or life, it wasn't happening around us. And at that time that was true. She didn't prohibit Rani from going to Mason's, and neither did my or Gus' parents after they received an accurate report from Mrs. Turner. Accurate in the sense that she reported what she had seen. She found the environment unfamiliar, didn't trust Mason, but hadn't seen anything illegal or immoral. Her mind was so much in the gutter, I guess she was expecting to see homosexual communists forcing innocent boys into indecent acts while drinking wine, smoking hashish, and farting on a Bible.

We arrived at Rani's house, the southeast corner townhouse at 56rd and Harper. Dr. Turner's study was on the ground level facing the front garden. Usually, he could be seen poring over books, manuscripts, making notes, or typing. He greeted us boys when we came and went, but rarely engaged in conversation. We thought that he thought that we were just too young and dumb. And we figured since he was getting older, he was busy with his work, and any teenage issues could be handled by his wife.

Dr. Turner was born in 1890. He was seventy-five during the Mason days– 1966 or so, while Lois Turner was barely forty. You see, they got married in Paris when Lois was around seventeen years old. I remember my mother saying that he was around thirty-five years older than Lois. Rani was born in 1948, and his older brother,

Lorenzo Jr., in 1945, the same year as my sister. Lois was essentially raising her sons, while Dr. Turner was perpetually occupied with his work. In her defense, I must say that she never experienced being a normal young woman. She was also raised along strict moral lines, often hypocritical, that was typical in better off, lighter skinned, Black nouveau bourgeois families during that time.

Lois, in my opinion, was over the edge. She was stingy, and domineering. She dressed her Rani and Lorenzo well, almost strictly from Brooks Brothers, as that was important for the family image. But, man, she was cheap. My mother said she had never seen a family with so much money, with children so skinny and malnourished looking. I remember if Rani asked his mother for fifty cents, his mother would respond with, "What happened to that dollar I gave you last week?" That's just one example. When my mother would take us all out, treat us, Rani ate like he hadn't had a real meal in months.

You said that there was nothing weird with Mason at that time. So did things change?

Indeed, they did. One thing is that we were getting older, and Mason was becoming more detached from his code of conduct around us. Mason had a friend by the name of Jim January who was also known as Panama Jim. Jim was a drug dealer, libertine, quasi-scholar, who had attended Shimer College along with Mason. Most of Mason's inner circle had attended Shimer College in Mt. Carroll, Illinois, and then moved to Chicago. Shimer was considered highly experimental by typical standards in its heyday, back in the sixties. There was concentration on Great Books as teachers, not professors or textbooks about Great Books. The works of Aristotle, Kafka, Nietzsche, Machiavelli, Shakespeare, de Beauvoir, da Vinci, and others were discussed in the form of Socratic dialogue between students. A professor stepped in only if needed. It was, and is, in no way like any traditional college: no Ivory Tower, entitled frat boys, and drunken spring-break date rapes. But most of the students were from privileged backgrounds.

Sadly, our dear friend, Rani, got caught in the grips of the unique Shimer demons and lost his mind. During Mason's time, and most unfortunately, Rani Turner's, the use of drugs was widespread, with heavy emphasis on psychedelics like LSD and mescaline. The Shimer world of Great Books, drugs, sex, and free-thinking, as extolled by Mason, Jim January, and others, had an irreversible, damaging influence on Rani. Gus and I were influenced, but mostly intrigued by the Shimer stories. But Rani, he went the distance. He convinced his parents that Shimer was what he wanted and would be good for him, and thus, began his sad and troubling future in and out of mental institutions and halfway houses.

You lost a friend?

I did, forever, at least in this world. Rani was my first friend. I had known him all my life. You see, my mother and Lois' mother, a woman I just knew as Mrs. Morton, were close friends. In fact, Rani introduced me to Gus when I was fourteen. As of now, that's fifty-two years ago.

What else happened as Mason detached from his code of conduct?

This Mason thing went from 1964 until 1967. Rani started at Shimer in fall of 1966. That's the same year that I left home for the first time and went to Boston. When I returned, I didn't see him until winter had set in, and he was acting strangely. On a visit to Chicago he was worried that his mother would find his cigarettes, so he asked me to keep them while he went home for a minute. I'm thinking, this is crazy, he's living on his own. He became terribly paranoid about many things, but especially his mother, who as I said, was stingy and domineering. That same winter, now 1967, Gus and I went to visit him at Shimer. There we had a light touch of the Shimer experience as guests. We met a character, one of Rani's acid buddies, by the name of Crick. Crick appropriately rhymes with prick, which is what that fellow was. He had Rani in a drug strangle hold. He was a vain, arrogant, little blond white guy who clearly resented our visit. It was immediately clear that Rani was in trouble. Crick had become a kind of parental figure to Rani. Crick, who had no experience in life, had seduced Rani into letting him become his LSD trip guide. Some people's brains, minds, are not engineered to deal with psychedelic drugs. Some run a higher risk of a bad trip, or "Trip of no Return" than others. There are many, many factors to be considered when one decides to explore the layers of the mind. One of the worst things a person can do is put their mind in the hands of a lame, know-nothing child who thinks that it's all just about getting some kicks and dominating someone who should be seeking professional or at least competent help for their problems.

In the spring of 1967, Rani became a patient at Manteno State Hospital, amental institution near Chicago that is now closed. I went to see him once, and he was completely removed from any sense of reality– that was saddening and disturbing. Even more disturbing were the fucking ignorant doctors' total lack of knowledge about psychedelics, the spiritual practices of certain indigenous people, and the whole drug scene that was sweeping across the western hemisphere. I tried to give clues and insights about what might be going on in Rani's head since I knew him, and was aware of many issues surrounding his life and family. They did not want to hear about it. The practice of psychiatry, at least at that time, was replete with stubborn, arrogant, well-paid practitioners who were clueless about the popular culture of an entire generation. I walked away praying that Rani would bounce back on his own... That never happened.

Did you ever see Rani again?

I did. Let me just fast forward briefly. Around 1980, I was walking with my son, Kevin, along Clark Street across from Lincoln Park in Chicago. Suddenly, stepping out of a doorway, which was a halfway house, was Rani. I said, "Rani, Rani Turner, is that you?" He gave me a long look and said, "Beau, come on up to my room a minute." He spoke to me as though I had seen him just the other day. We went to his room. A bed, nightstand, some clothes strewn over chairs, jars of peanut butter and jam, a television, and a radio. Nothing else really. This was the room of someone who is given medication then sleeps. Maybe goes for a walk, eats, then sleeps some more—for years and years. His teeth were yellow and rotten from years of medication. Other than that, he looked pretty much the same. On the way down the steps from the fourth floor to the exit, Rani kept repeating the same phrase over and over: "I'm aware, I'm aware, I'm aware." Over and over. I knew that Rani was locked into one of those painful, confusing, and probably inescapable LSD transition points that I'd seen before. And so, I say to our readers, bluntly: Leave that shit alone, because nobody knows the makeup of their brain, and nobody knows how their brain is going to react. And when you buy street drugs, ain't no telling what that shit is.

Anything else happen during Mason's moral shift?

A lot happened. Mason moved to different apartments, all in Hyde Park. Slowly, his intellectual friends were replaced by unsavory drug dealers and hangers-on. He seemed to be trapped in some sort of post LSD trip psychological dilemma. He stopped playing chess, and he had been a highly-rated player. He got a girlfriend, an ugly brute named Beverly, who was twice his size. But really, it was her personality that was so wretched, not her size. There was nothing beautiful inside that woman. She hated everybody and was a vocal racist. When Mason decided to have Beverly and those other characters around, I knew he was on the verge of some type of mental collapse. At some point when Gus and I were out of Chicago, he had a breakdown. Eventually, he and Beverly left Chicago and went to his hometown of Rockford, Illinois.

Did you ever hear anything else about him?

In 1987, I was at the Printers Row Book Fair in Chicago. And just walking along I saw Mason selling books and records from his shop in Rockford, Illinois, Toad Hall Books and Records. Gruesome-ass Beverly was there as well. It was a pleasure seeing him after twenty years. Time does change people, hopefully for the better, and Mason looked well. Beverly hadn't changed. Still bitter and inhospitable. Well, we re-hooked up. As a man now, 38 years old, our way of interacting had certainly changed. I had traveled extensively, lived in many cultures, and had become quite worldly. Larry had immersed himself in his great loves: books, art, and literature. And he did it in a Rockford bookshop that consisted of thirteen rooms. Of Beverly, he said, "She's an indolent slob."

Around 2005, sadly, Larry passed, and within a year Beverly also passed. They left their collections to the world. They had no heirs.

That's a good story from your Hyde Park world. Now you've been dealing on two fronts and are maturing through experiences that many people don't have until later in life, if at all. You haven't said anything specific about the ladies in your life; what was happening with them?

Okay. One August day in 1965, I got on a scale at Rosenblum's Drugstore and Soda Fountain, up on 71st and Merrill, and weighed 325 pounds. You know, black kids don't mess around when it comes to signifying. I was tired of being called names like "fat ass" and "high pockets, "and getting made fun of in front of girls by neighborhood idiots. I decided to lose weight quickly. I asked my mother for help, as she cooked and was a professional Home Economist. I choose a diet that was called the Drinking Man's Diet, and the Air Force Diet. Today, there is a similar diet called the Dr. Atkins Diet. It's all about eating less carbohydrates. I started my diet that same day. By Christmas I was down to 250, and by May, man, I was under 200 pounds.

This is May of 1966, the year I made my first extended exit from home. I went to Boston where my sister was studying at Boston University. She had invited me to come and stay with her for a while because I was not doing well at home. In fact, it had become obvious to me and my parents as well that I did not have many more days to live at home. I just craved independence.

When I got to Boston I had my reshaped body. I was in great physical condition as well. For the first time in my life I was fitting into the acceptable size norm. It didn't take long for me to figure out that normal is just some made up bullshit. Lord knows how many normal looking people I've met with have souls the size of a pin head. Up until this point, like most young boys, my friends and I bragged about things we had not done with girls. We just told each other lies that resembled what older guys, grown men, had told us they had done, which were mostly lies. But now, I was getting them looks from the ladies– from college girls around Cambridge, the sisters over in Roxbury, and everybody in between. I was seventeen, tall, thin, handsome, and looking around twenty-five or so. I was never carded throughout my life, except by a goddamn fool working in a 7-11 convenience store in Chicago when I was sixty years old. So, I could go into any kind of nightclub or liquor store without a problem.

But I had to shake the *hanx*. I was a virgin. The morning after the first night at my sister's place, Kristy, one of her roommates, climbed into my bed. Now, I would not have had a problem with that except for the fact that she had spent the night in a room next to mine with her boyfriend. I heard them in there hollering and moaning all night. Then, as soon as the boyfriend left in the morning, she came to my bed. I wasn't having it. I was not going to let this girl Georgia me. I had partially grown up in the street-wise philosophy of pimps and whores, where that kind of behavior was strictly forbidden and relegates you to the status of a trick. *Can't let no woman just take some dick.* At the very least, the actions must be mutual, or some kind of business. Also, this was the middle of the Free Love Era, and I just wasn't at that place in my thinking. Kristy left my bed disappointed, but more respectful of me than when she had climbed in. Later, at breakfast, she suggested that she introduce me to a friend of hers, Marjorie.

I met Marge that very same day. She was tall and Rubenesque with dark brown curly hair, almost like an Afro, which is characteristic of some Caucasian-looking people that are a blend. Marge was of Italian Jewish heritage mixed with something she wasn't sure about. The result was a very attractive person. We were introduced on the phone, and met later for coffee at the Hayes-Bickford cafeteria near Harvard Square. We talked about jazz, the Blues, books, etcetera. Marge was a school teacher with interesting conversation. I just told creative lies mixed with some elements of truth. But at the end of the day, we both knew what we wanted. Not to be too obvious, and showing a little restraint, I invited her to have dinner with me, confident that she would decline and invite me to her house. That's exactly what happened. She suggested that she could put a little dinner together at her place. Into a taxi, and out to Brookline we went. Not with much food, but several glasses of wine later, we were in bed. Uh, this is when things got embarrassingly awkward for me. None of the lies told to me by them ignorant friends of mine panned out, and none of the naked pictures and movies I had seen prepared me for the moment. Man, I had no idea what I was doing. Outside of a strip club, I'd never been in a room with a naked woman before, and never been naked myself outside of bathing. Here we are laying in the bed kissing. Marge gently urged me to take the lead and climb on top of her. I did. Then she moved the whole of me forward, upward towards her face until I was directly above her mouth. Marge engaged me with passionate vigor. The she pushed me back down so that I might enter her. I couldn't find my way. That's when she said, "Ah, Sweetie, you're a virgin?" I admitted that I was, and simultaneously lost all semblance of an erection. But not for long. Marge was patient and knowledgeable. I certainly appreciate her schooling my young ass.

The night rolled on: wine, reefer, all the positions. But I didn't kiss her below the navel, and barely touched her breasts. Why? Because of ignorant and idiotic notions, I had learned from friends and dumb-ass grown men. I was shackled by myths, taboos, and lies. The "go-to" people for sex education should be one's parents. But my parents, like many, were just as shackled as I was. Nobody would dare speak about anything regarding sex. When a woman was pregnant they lowered their voices when speaking about it, as though the mere mention of it might suggest to anyone within earshot that *they* were immoral in some way, or guilty by association.

Well, in summer of 1966 I was seventeen years old, and had my first lover. Marge wanted us to live together, but I was protecting her from what might happen if the wrong people found out my true age. You see, I told Marge that I was twenty-one, and she believed me. Twenty-one was an important number back then, because a male was not considered grown in some states until that age. Marge was twenty-three, and I didn't want her to have any kind of trouble because of me. Also, Massachusetts had Blue Laws on the books regarding cohabitation with black males. I moved out of my sister's place, which had three white women living there, and got my own place, a $20-a-week room over on Huntington Avenue in Boston. I felt like I had to protect myself from co-habitation laws and protect Marge from possible statutory rape. Having my own crib was essential, even though I spent a lot of time at Marge's.

You were right in being concerned about statutory rape charges against her, and some kind of prosecution of you may have been possible?

That's right. Probably, nothing would have happened to her, but those wicked laws were designed specifically for the black man to be prosecuted, found guilty, and imprisoned. Today, she may have gotten into serious trouble. For sure sexual misconduct, pedophilia, and any abuse of children is absolutely revolting, and perpetrators should be punished to the full extent of the law. But, I could not imagine myself turning in Marge, or any other adult woman I was with prior to being "legally" grown. In those days, different states had different laws regarding the age of consent. In one state, you were a statutory rapist, in another, a respectable citizen on a date. I find troubling these young men in the news who are now in their twenties claiming that a woman had sex with them when they were seventeen. I was just fine knowing those women, and I wish I had known more. Of course, if theywere taken advantage of, that's another matter. It's hard to believe that a guy two months from his eighteenth birthday is being taken advantage of by an eighteen-year-old young woman as some have claimed.

After your affair with Marge?

I went back to Chicago in September of 1966 and planned my extended exit from Chicago, and the United States, along with Gus. Between then and December 1967, I had a steady girlfriend, Marlena, and a couple of flings here and there. Some people called Marlena the "Chicken Hawk" because she had bird legs and was said by my neighborhood buddies to look like a cartoon character with the same name.

Now you are hanging in two different worlds. Did you ever try to bring the two together?

I moved back and forth quite a bit because of the different vibes. But Gus and I had our sights on a complete change from Chicago. So we sort of hunkered down into a "let's get the fuck out of Chicago/America" mode. We had done some traveling back and forth to Boston, Canada. We had night-clubbed and partied across Chicago. We had been caught up in riots and protests. We had pretty much driven our parents crazy. Also, my neighborhood was becoming more and more dangerous. Gang wars erupted between the Blackstone Rangers, Disciples, Vice Lords, and others. Jeff Fort consolidated the Blackstone Ranger affiliates and the Disciples into a new criminal organization he founded called the El Rukns. They had cash and political muscle via the typical corrupt Chicago avenues. Fort was quite an organizer. Had he used his talents for positive endeavors, I believe he could have been a highly successful entrepreneur, social organizer, and a voice for change.

Killings increased in my neighborhood. My parents and sister had gotten mugged. I implored them to please move, but my father was too stubborn. I tried to include Jibbs, my friend who got shot in the mouth, in some of our plans, but he just couldn't see himself outside of America. Gus and I took him on a short trip to Canada once and he was overwhelmed by change. Violently so. Wanted to fight because he could not speak French. He had been my last connection to my neighborhood, and Rani, my oldest friend and Hyde Parker, was now institutionalized. These things, among others, like the duping of the American people with the war in Vietnam, became too fucked-up of a vibe to want to be around.

On December 29, 1967, the time had come for the Great Goodbye, as we called it. That date happened to be my mother's birthday. She was sixty-one years old.

Where did you go, and how did you get there?

Our destination was Québec City. Our mission was to read Great Books, learn to write, enjoy life, and to come to know another culture. We traveled by rail on the Canadian National Railroad from Chicago's Polk Street station to Toronto, then from Toronto to Montreal, and from Montreal to Québec City. With a stopover in Montreal, the journey took about three days. The trip was uneventful, but our imaginations were boundless as we romanticized about what might happen on our great adventure.

One thing that happened, though, was when we arrived at the Canadian Border, and had to explain to the Customs official why we had boxes of books and phonograph records if we were tourists. I said some things were gifts with no value, and that the other items are necessary for our personal enjoyment. The Customs agent smiled and said, "Welcome to Canada. Enjoy your stay." In those days Canada welcomed those who were opposed to the Vietnam War, and who were doing battle in the streets and courts of the United States to achieve equal rights and justice. Fifty years on, the battle continues.

This was the dead of winter, but we, as literary romantics, thought of ourselves as hearty young men who could stand up to the elements without a problem. We convinced ourselves that if Boris

Pasternak's wimpy Doctor Zhivago could handle the tundra between Varykino and Yuriatin, going back and forth to see his Lara, we hearty young Bluesmen could handle the equally frigid Canadian winter. Our resolve was often put to the test.

Y'all must have been quite a sight to the locals?

Ah, yes. We were in no way a usual sight. We had on greenish, nearly ankle-length World War One Army coats that Gus called trudgers, as in trudging across the Canadian terrain. We had serious lumberjack boots, sweaters, scarves, wooly caps, gloves: we were ready. I remember one day we were walking along Rue Sainte-Jean, a major street in Québec, when suddenly we noticed nearly everyone on a crowded bus was looking and pointing at us. People had gotten up and crossed the aisle in the bus to see us. To see the *les Noir.* I mean, the bus was visibly leaning as riders were gaping out of the windows on the same side.

What about money and a place to live?

Oh, we had a few dollars when we arrived, enough to rent a large room in a rooming house and buy food for three months. We rented an L-shaped room at 60 Rue Sainte-Ursule, top floor. Now the rent, that was $20 a week, and food and wine were cheap. After that, it was up to the Cosmics. The reality is that if you worry too much about money you'll never get certain things done. Many peo-ple don't have a relationship with the Cosmics, or positive forces, so they stop themselves before even get started early in life because of their ideas about money. Gus and I just had the desire to have ad-ventures, grow and change— and enjoy being young.

Back in those days there wasn't tourism like today?

These were the last years of the old, old Québec, before a huge tourism campaign began. The largest hotel I remember was the Chateau Frontenac, and most of the grocery shopping was done at the local depanneur. Alcohol was sold at government-owned liquor out-lets that resembled a car parts counter rather than a liquor shop. There was no browsing. Customers made selections from a form that listed inventory. You checked off what you wanted, gave the clerk the slip, and he would fetch your choice. There were no recommendations from the staff about anything. No wine tastings or publicity. And the hours were like a bank, nine to five, and a few hours on Saturday. The clerks were bored government drones working towards their pension. All of that has changed now. The government still runs the liquor business, but some of the shops are quite impressive with huge selections and occasional great bargains, and knowledgeable staff, with some of them enjoying their work.

We drank wine and ate good for a while. But for the most part we spent those winter months on Saint-Ursule engrossed in what we thought to be Great Books. Some authors and thinkers like Socrates, Plato, Marcus Aurelius, and many others whose thinking serves as a cornerstone for the development of European intellectualism were deleted from our must-read list, or relegated to being lower in the order of preference. Our library consisted of James Baldwin, Zora Neale Hurston, Langston Hughes, Richard Wright, James Weldon Johnson, Claude Brown, Ralph Ellison, and many other writers—some of the Harlem Renaissance, Negritude Movement, and more contemporary Black writers then like Amos Tutuola, Amiri Baraka, and Nikki Giovanni. And in those days we consulted occasionally with the I Ching. Also, the *Paris Review*, the *Partisan Review*, and other literary magazines were a part of our collection.

How about contemporary European writers?

Oh, yes. It was and is important to try to gain some insight into the minds of those who held us in bondage, as well as those who disagreed in principle to the system of repression. Those who influence every thought and tradition, ranging from clothing style to religion, from language to etiquette, and so on. After reading Herman Hesse's novels *Steppenwolf, Journey to the East*, and *Magister Ludi*, I begin to gain some understanding about the troublesome inner struggle present in the Euro-Psyche. A condition that I call Eurosis: the condition of Europeans struggling with tradition, entitlement, oppressive regimes, incest, elitism, racism, and the most sinister of institutions, the guilt and fear peddling Roman Catholic Church. Imagine, living in some shit called The Dark Ages, with the mostly illiterate masses controlled by royalty, military, and religion. The only solution, a revolution in everything. The result: new freedom and a rise of newer intellectuals, who in most cases continued to repress. It took strong and determined people to overcome so much. But this isn't a European history discussion. I'm digressing, excuse me.

No, that's cool. I mean it's certainly important to understand your process in coming to understand those who have had such an enormous influence.

It is interesting and sometimes humorous to read those looking for answers. Freud for one, on some issues is almost laughable to me as an African in the Americas, a black man. And in a way, that says so much about his struggles. His theories on sexual perversion, and infantile sexuality, and the Oedipus Complex, are based on observations and behavior within European cultures, whereas the cultures of native peoples around the globe have for the most part, respectful rituals of mating, marriage, childbirth, puberty, adulthood, aging, death, and beyond. Personally, I take exception to female mutilation. And I know women do also. So, there is not perfection in any tradition, and it's up to those matriarchs and patriarchs in those traditions to make the changes the people want. These highly spiritual traditions served the needs of many for thousands of years until encountering European conquerors and missionaries. The destructive result was almost immediate. But as chattels or former chattels, our psychological issues were never addressed or even considered. We were not human beings. Of course, we had to rely on the old traditions as much as possible: Voodoo, syncretic practices, and other forms of African and indigenous peoples' mysticism.

Native people were systematically stripped of their culture and forced to accept in some way the White's religions and values, that included rape of women and children, which is widely considered taboo by native cultures universally. And believe me, the European knew his shit was fucked-up; all they had to do was to look at their own history, especially in France, Spain, Portugal, England, and Germany. And some did, thankfully, but to not much avail, while others basked in arrogance and greed, creating shameful histories as they went along. I do respect Freud, Jung, and Fromm, a critic of Freud. Debate is a good thing. Some philosophers and novelists as well searched for answers to the European struggle. Schopenhauer is a pleasure to read from time-to-time. I don't like his "On Women," but I rather like another short piece, "On Noise." The nervous Kierkegaard, a man who seemed tormented by his thoughts on sin and Christianity, penned an excellent piece that I enjoy reading, "The

Present Age." But most European philosophers and great writers shared one common delusion, and that is that white people are superior.

Poor things. Who are your favorite writers now, and who would you recommend reading?

Favorites can easily fade away. Right now, I'm thinking about Toni Morrison, Maya Angelou, Anais Nin, Henry Miller, Alejo Carpentier, Jorge Luis Borges, Rabindranath Tagore, J. Krishnamurti, J.P. Donleavy, Henry Dumas, Alexander Pushkin, Alexander Dumas, and Gabriel Garcia Marquez. I have been rereading some of these works, and I'm using some of them in my teaching syllabus at Harper College.

The picture of your Québec days is getting clearer. What did you do when the money ran out?

The lack of funds almost became problematic in April. For about a week we lived on oatmeal, coffee, and beans. Then on an unusually warm spring day while strolling along the boardwalk that's situated in front of the Chateau Frontenac, Gus and I exchanged glances with three young ladies: Micheline, Lise, and Janet. I pulled out my harmonica and played a few notes. That got their attention. "*Ohhh, c'est bon la musique . . .continue, s'il vous plait*," requested Micheline. And I did, and then we sat on a bench and stumbled through some French, and they attempted to use their classroom English. We all struggled, but we communicated. And we're all just loving it! This was a kind of storybook meeting, as were the months that followed. We explained that we were writers and Bluesmen, in Québec to escape the trammels of life in the United States like discrimination, riots, police brutality, the Vietnam war, and more. And they told us that they were high school students, in *l'ecole secondaire*. The girls said that they were eighteen, but we didn't believe them. They later confessed that they were sixteen. And you know, coming from the States, we were extremely cautious hanging out with these girls as we didn't want to be accused of violating some law regarding underage girls, especially white ones, and we didn't want to get them into trouble. We talked and talked, stumbling through topics struggling in French and English. We agreed to meet again on the boardwalk, but during our conversation, we mentioned our room on Rue Sainte-Ursule. The next morning, a Sunday, we finished the last of the oatmeal and navy beans. I decided to go out on the boardwalk and play a little harp and sing for tips. I didn't get far. As was about to exit the front door, I encountered Micheline and Lise about to ring the landlady's bell who would let in visitors. I was amazed. The girls had two bags of groceries and wine that they had taken from their parents' cave– and an Edith Piaf LP as gifts. Up the stairs we went. Gus was trying to eat what was left of some uncooked oatmeal flakes. He was astounded. To this day, that meal with Micheline and Lise stands out as the most memorable of my life. It was simple, but nourishing. The company was great, and the experience was completely new... different from anything we had experienced. We were experiencing some of the beauty of Québec culture and its people.

What delights did they bring?

There was a variety of cheeses, some local and some from France. Pate, sausages, baguettes, butter, roast pork and chicken, jam, cans of beans and soups, coffee, tea, fresh cream, and six bottles of wine. It all felt good– the company, the wine, the food, and the freedom I never experienced in the United States. Here we were, with new friends having a great time in our 100-square foot, L-shaped room, listening to Muddy Waters, Sonny Boy Williamson, John Coltrane, and Esther Phillips. What was hep about albums is that they also served as décor and cool visuals. Large images of our favorite artists in the form of LP covers were placed throughout the room. Cannot do that with flash drives.

Around six in the evening Micheline and Lise had to leave to be sure get the bus to Sainte-Foy, a suburb where they lived. The bus station was on Rue Sainte-Jean. We offered to walk them to the bus, but they said no. Later, we found out that nothing goes unnoticed in Québec City. If we had walked with them to the bus, somebody who knew their families would have observed, reported, and embellished what they had seen. And so, they left. All was quite innocent. Nothing happened except food, conversation, music, and laughter. Youth! How sweet it can be!

You had food and wine, but you were still broke?

Yes, but as I said, one must have faith in the Cosmics, the

Creator's beacons, if you will. We had no money, and for a few days we didn't need any. We had books, music, and food. And a few extra rolls of toilet paper. All good.

One morning, three or four days later, Gus and I were out for a walk along Rue Sainte-Louis. Coming into view and walking directly towards us was an elegantly dressed black couple. He was maybe six feet tall and slender, and she was average size and quite attractive. I thought them to be in their mid-fifties.

You know when many Americans travel abroad, they yearn to run into someone who speaks English. When we were all close to one another on the street, the man asked if we spoke English. And since we do speak English, a conversation ensued. The couple turned out to be Reverend and Mrs. William James– the same William James that author Claude Brown gives thanks to in the introduction to his bestselling book *Manchild in the Promised Land*. The same Reverend James that Pastored the Metropolitan Methodist Church in Harlem. Reverend James knew all the ins and outs of being black in America. We sat down with him for hours. We learned about his work through his church in Harlem, and told him our ambitions and how we were going about achieving them. Reverend James was a huge supporter of the arts and Chairperson of the Harlem Urban Development Corporation. He was recognized for his life's work by a formal declaration of the U.S. Congress. When we met, he was already an established heavyweight who just kept getting heavier.

He wanted to see where we lived. It was a bit embarrassing, but we showed him. He was a little bit shocked to see how we were living. "Bohemian," he called our lifestyle, but he was not harsh or disapproving. They were leaving the next day, and he asked if it would be okay for him to stop by before he left. The next morning, Reverend James came by and invited us to come to Harlem, and eventually work as counselors at a camp his church sponsored in Pennsylvania. And he said for us not to feel obligated, it was just an offer, and we would be paid a salary. Then he handed me an envelope and said not to open it until after he left. As soon as he was in his car, I opened the envelope. Five hundred dollars. The Cosmics. Faith in the Creator, and your best effort. That's it, like Pharaoh Sanders says, "The Creator has a master plan." One just must recognize that goodness.

Beau, that's relying on the spirits and having them come through for you. Did you go to Harlem and work for Reverend James?

I made a trip to Harlem, but did not go to work for him. I stayed in his home for two days, and enjoyed great hospitality and conversation mostly about black survival, civil rights, and the various efforts he was making in the community. He introduced me to several high profile Harlemites including Congressman Adam Clayton Powell, who visited his home while I was there.

One thing stands out about Reverend James. At no point, did he ever mention religion. Not in Québec or in Harlem. He never attempted to sway me with his beliefs. In fact, he never said what he believed. I gathered that his Church was useful for him to accomplish what he wanted the community and for himself.

Was he disappointed?

No, and he didn't seem disappointed or surprised. But I was truthful. I told him that I had completely different ideas about how I wanted to help my people, and being at a camp in Pennsylvania had absolutely no appeal. I said I hoped to live my life in such a way that when I became older I would be regarded as an example of independence and accomplishment. I was nineteen; he had already seen my poverty-stricken, eccentric way of living in Québec, so he did concur that maybe my calling was of a different nature. He also said that he had never encountered young men like Gus and me before. He appreciated my visit. I had made visiting a priority to get to know him better. And to express my gratitude for the help he had given us.

Did you go to New York only to see Reverend James?

Yes. The New York portion of the trip was to see him. Gus and I would take occasional excursions down to the U.S. during our Québec days. Sometimes we'd fly, other times take the Greyhound, hitchhike, or share a ride with a student maybe that was traveling to the U.S. On this occasion, I hitchhiked to Montreal, then took a bus to Boston to see friends, then I caught a ride to and from New York through rideshare hook-up.

How did you leave things with Reverend James?

He wished me well and sent his regards to Gus. He told me that the door would always be open if I wanted to come back, if only to visit. Over the next few months we exchanged letters, and eventually the communication ceased. But William James was a person who gave much, and he was one of the few people that I've met in my life who helped and supported what I was doing without wanting something in return. I think his camp offer was because he thought Gus and I could have a positive role in his work. I suggest interested readers check him out, and author Claude Brown, one of the many he helped.

What did you do after you left Reverend James' home?

I went back to Boston for a couple of days and hung out with friends. I caught Muddy Waters at the jazz workshop on Boylston Street one evening. The band was smoking. It was Otis Spann on piano, Sammy Lawhorn and Luther "Snake Boy" Johnson on guitars, Sonny Wimberley on bass, S.P. Leary on drums, and George Smith on harmonica. This was a great Muddy Waters Band. Then I hit the Boston Tea Party on Berkeley Street, a psychedelic-lighted converted meeting hall like the Fillmore East in New York and Paradiso in Amsterdam. A friend, Peter Wolfe, who later gained fame as lead singer with the J. Geils Band, had a radio show on WBCN radio that was located in the Tea Party. Back in those days one could see a major act for $4.50 to $5, tops. And that was for the likes of Joe Cocker, Pink Floyd, the Allman Brothers, Santana, Taj Mahal, Lou Reed, Buddy Guy, and Charlie Musselwhite, as a small example. Hanging out at the Tea Party was big fun. It didn't take long to meet a young lady and end up flopping at her crib for a day or two. It was a time when the free love movement was the thing. Birth control pills probably outsold Coca-Cola.

That's what I did, and Gus also, again and again. Swoop down to the States: party, enjoy music, ladies, visit with literary contacts like Argentinean creative genius, Jorge Luis Borges, and maybe even work for a minute. Then return to the quieter life in Québec City for a period of study, writing, and practicing music.

I'm curious, and certainly are readers are about your times with Borges.

The Borges sessions were in 1967, when Borges was visiting lecturer at Harvard University. Gus and I met Borges through Norman Thomas di Giovanni, who would eventually collaborate with and translate much of Borges' writing. His relationship with Borges had, and I believe still has, many twist and turns—some legal, regarding Borges' widow and his literary estate, and some involving deep envy within the community of academics associated with Borges. However, initially, we just wanted to meet the man who possessed such an incredible imagination. During the first conversation with Borges, he asked who were some of our favorite writers. We talked about a few black writers—Langston Hughes, James Baldwin, Leroi Jones, Frantz Fanon, and others. But when Nigerian author Amos Tutuola was mentioned, that was a writer he was unfamiliar with. I told him about Tutuola's imagination. The beings he created and his treatment of language, time, space, and Yoruba mysticism. Borges, being nearly totally blind, asked if we would mind reading Tutuola to him. Of course not. We had two more meetings at where he was living near Concord Avenue, not far from Harvard Square in Cambridge. At each of those sessions Gus and I took turns reading from *The Palm Wine Drinkard*, a novel by Tutuola. Borges loved Tutuola's humor and total command of a language created by him. He said not many writers had command of alternative realities. Tutuola's formal education ended around sixth grade, but he is a master word crafter. These sessions were among the most rewarding times of my young life, and Borges said they were rewarding for him as well. Unfortunately, there were only two sessions because of Borges' schedule. I was eighteen at the time.

That's the way to move forward, not only meeting the people you want to meet, but also having some meaningful interaction. Great recollection. Moving on, how about swoops in and out of Boston. Did you ever pause from adventure and fun to earn money?

I had several jobs. Stuffing fiberglass into speakers for Acoustic Research. Making rifles. And I didn't even know what I was making. I just pulled a lever down when a piece of metal came down the conveyer belt. I was a security guard and got fired for turning on the Mars lights and the siren and speeding through red lights, which was something mischievous I had always wanted to do. I worked in a bookbindery. I parked cars for a guy named Moe on Wall Street, got fired for denting a Rolls-Royce. I did all sorts of day labor that paid at the end of the work day, including mopping floors and cleaning toilets in the Revlon Building in Manhattan and at Northeastern University in Boston. I worked in the steel mills. I worked in the merchandising department of a major bank. LaBosse, these are just a few.

Getting out and making a few dollars was very much part of your program. In a way, part of your freedom.

Very much so. To be able to earn money is a level of freedom. Getting paid fairly is another matter. I wanted to move around as I pleased. But I ain't gone lie, I hated most of those jobs, but I did what had to be done at the time.

One of the oddest and disturbing things that happened on a job was when Greece, a friend from Chicago, and I got a job with a black-owned company, Owens Movers and Storage in Cambridge in spring of '68. We got fired for talking to white girls. Mr. Owens, about fifty years old, had the contract to move young women from their dorm rooms at Radcliffe College to a storage facility. His hiring was part of a "support local and minority businesses: initiative. The moving crew were all black men. Most of them were laborers by day, drunks by night, according to their own self-proclamations. The move was indeed labor. But it didn't take long for Greece and me to establish a rapport with some of the ladies. And it made sense since as we were all around the same age. We moved books and spoke about books. We moved boxes of LP's and talked about music. By the time lunchtime came, Greece and I had been having pleasant conversations with several of the ladies who invited us to lunch with them. Our fellow movers were jealous and afraid of white people. They went back and told Mr. Owens that we were talking with and even ate with white girls. Owens wasted no time chastising us when we showed up for work the next morning: "Y'all know good and goddamn well you ain't supposed to be messin' around with no white gals no place, no how," he ranted. "Take you motherfuckin' checks and don't bring you asses around here no mo!" We knew Mr. Owens was not only too irate to speak about the situation, but also too conditioned in his thinking. We didn't offer any explanation. We just took our twenty-five dollars apiece and headed on down the line.

Well, not that he had to be, but being in the business he was in,

you wouldn't expect him to understand where you and Greece were at in yours. Even though those were tough days, it was possible to have some kind of rapport with your own generation. But for him, given his generation, you must have been incomprehensibly out of line. And for the guys that worked for him as well.

At the time, I thought it bizarre to be hired and fired by a black man for speaking to a white woman. Had he been white, that would have been perfectly understandable. Back then we laughed it off and felt a bit sorry for him. But the situation could have been different. He could have been right. Had it been another school, not the socially liberal Harvard–Radcliffe complex, we may have gotten into big trouble, the kind he was worried about.

For sure. If my memory serves me correctly, Cambridge had extremes, from liberal campuses to out-and-out racist police who had it in for students. You know, they saw the students as rich kids, and Black sympathizers and themselves as hardworking blue-collar types and underpaid civil servants. A lot of jealousy there. What other jobs?

I had a job at an Interior Design firm called Trade Winds on Newbury Street in Boston, delivering samples to wealthy clients in Milton, Marblehead, and other affluent Boston suburbs. I was supposed to politely drop off the samples and leave. But invariably, some of the bored, tipsy, and horny housewives would ask me my thoughts on a pattern or fabric. When they asked me to please sit down for coffee, tea, or a drink, I did. And why not? I knew the job was going to be short-lived, so why not enjoy. I had no idea what I was talking about. I just made up stuff or pivoted off what they were saying, as in, "I agree with you, the Persian Brocades are far more durable." I did end up in the sack with one of them though, Gertrude, an attractive, redheaded, fiftyish, Pol Roget-consuming recent widow.

My downfall came when one of the ladies called the design company and said she wanted to order something that I had suggested. The owners obliged her but fired me. How dare I, a Negro delivery man, have any kind of conversation with their prestigious clients? My firing was swift, rude, and laced with haughty disdain for my black ass. Before leaving I said, "I been fuckin' some of them ladies, so it just could be that I'll tell them they should cancel all your shit." Then I demanded my pay up to the second. They said they would send my check. Nope. I wanted my money right then and there. I threatened them with calling in the Black Panthers, who I didn't know, and told them I didn't think they wanted to go through the embarrassment of having it made public that they refused to pay a black man, and under what circumstances. They gave me my money. About a week later, I gave Gertrude a call. We agreed to meet at the bar at the Ritz Hotel near the Boston Commons.

Beau, did you have the proper attire for the Ritz?

Indeed, I did. I always travelled with what Gus and I called survival essentials: several silk paisley and stripped neckties; two ascots; a sports coat; dress trousers; four essential Brooks Brothers dress shirts in blue, stone, pink, and white; and rugged, but dressy boots or shoes. Exactly what's needed for certain occasions. In fact, at Trade Winds, being well dressed was a requirement.

Gertrude and I met and passed a lovely afternoon. We talked about what had happened to me at Trade Winds, and she came up with a scheme to punish the bastards and have some fun.

This is what we did. Gertrude called Trade Winds and told them she would like a meeting to help with her decisions and to finalize her order. She insisted that John Brown, the forty-something, ultra-thin, blonde-hair-in-place, prissy little manager come himself as she could possibly be spending a great deal of money. The doorbell chimed around ten in the morning. Gertrude answered the door wearing a sexy, but not too revealing pink, silky morning gown. She invited Brown in and served him coffee in her dining room size kitchen. Brown pulled out samples of wall coverings, etcetera, and spread them around the table. I was peeping from the library waiting for my cue to enter. Brown was working her, trying to close, when she said, "Let me call my other half in to have a look along with me. Darling, can you come?" That was my cue. I waited about 30 seconds then I made my entry. I entered wearing a silk paisley dressing gown with royal blue pajamas underneath. Courtesy of her late husband. "How nice of you to drop by, Mr. Brown." Then Gertrude and I shared a lengthy good morning kiss. I said to Brown,

"I told Gertrude that at Trade Winds, only you possess the expertise to aid in our decision making. Isn't that so?" He stuttered, turned whiter, then red. He was overcome with shock, anger, and confusion, all of which he tried to conceal. "Are you okay my boy?" I asked. He had to be careful here because Gertrude was well connected and had provided several referrals in the past.

John Brown squirmed. He was angry but couldn't say what he was thinking. Finally, he said, "I must say this is most unusual," coughing altissimo. "Indeed, it is, for you maybe. But let's move forward with the business," I said. Over the next half-hour or so we looked at samples; Gertrude thumbed through a catalog of graphic art that Brown suggested for the recreation room. I denounced everything as cheap replicas of Miro, Dali, Gauguin, and old movie posters. "These will never do and they are overpriced!" I declared. I know the wholesale price of Dali reproductions can be a little as five dollars, and some appear to be signed and numbered. But usually it's a forged signature and made-up A.P. Some shady art dealers, interior decorators, and others buy them from publishers and wholesalers that the public is unaware of. For example, the often-duplicated Dali pieces, *Slave Market with a Disappearing Bust of Voltaire* and *Lincoln in Dalivision,* can be found today for under twenty dollars. The internet has forced art scoundrels to straighten up somewhat. Previously, the public didn't have easy access to such information. The hustle is still out there, but there is much more awareness among buyers.

John Brown wanted to sell a Dali Serigraph, framed, for around two thousand dollars, and insisted that that was a fair and discounted price. I knew that was a markup of 900 percent. I said, "Naw, motherfucker, we ain't goin for it! "He actually got in my face and said to me, "Beg your pardon. How dare you speak to me that way!" I responded, "Motherfucker, I say what I want in my house." "I don't think this is your house," he said with a smirk. Gertrude inserted, "You've got it wrong, Mr. Brown, this is *our* house. That means his house. And I believe what my man is telling me about your prices, and I know how you've treated him. I think you should try to be the sophisticated person that you present yourself to be, and apologize, then leave."

Brown gathered his samples, catalogs, etcetera and without any gesture of apology, or good bye to his client and referral source, he haughtily headed towards the front door, making short, quick steps. Before he was out I said, "You really are a seasoned asshole...pun intended." Brown tried to stare me down. I feel back on one heel, street style, and said, "I'll knock them whiteheads off your forehead." Gertrude, who was drinking her fourth or fifth mimosa, cracked up uncontrollably. Brown, having surpassed our hopes of seeing him agitated, left.

Sweet, sweet Gertrude and I rolled around for a couple of hours, then she took me to Logan Airport, where thanks to her, I had a first-class trip to Montreal.

Man, y'all get him good. Put Brown in his place. Now going back to your New York trip, and back through Boston, you were talking about flopping with a woman you met at the Tea Party. Shall we continue from there?

Let me consolidate a bit here. Yeah, I flopped with a lady for a couple of days. But the reality is that Gus and I had numerous flops around the Boston area. We had girlfriends who attended Brandeis University. They lived in a semi-dorm called The Castle because of its design. And there were the McKenzie sisters, Jalene and Jalina, over in Roxbury. They were exceptionally fun ladies: jet black, musical, mid-twenties, stomp-down sisters who loved to party. Only problem at their crib was the occasional visit by Jesse, their younger brother, and his buddies, who were young wannabe pimps and talked a world of shit: "My hoes, them hoes..." And there were other flops from Beacon Hill to Somerville. Now occasionally, we would rent a room on Saint Botolph street near Prudential Plaza, where I parked cars occasionally. In those days, like in Quebec City, one could rent a furnished room for $20 to $30 a week.

I was staying in one of those rooms the day Martin Luther King was assassinated. I remember I was having a rather animated conversation about the rent with Cecile Nichols, the sixtyish, squatty, drunken, red-faced balding landlord, when a group of angry black men came running down the street. When they saw me speaking with him, they wanted to know if everything was alright. They wanted to fuck-up some white people. Man, Cecile's drunk ass started talking shit: "Don't come on my property!" I saved his dumb drunk ass. I pleaded with them brothers not to fuck him up. I said: "He just a dumb-ass, drunk old white man. Please don't pay him no attention. And don't make no trouble for y'all selves and me, because you know, today is about anger. We gotta get through it to continue the struggle."

Were they cool with that?

They were. They huffed on up to Massachusetts Avenue which was flooded with protesters. Terrible day, April 4, 1968. Then on May 23, 1968, writer, teacher, and civil rights activist Henty Dumas got murdered in cold-blood by a New York City transit policeman at the 125th street subway station up in Harlem. A few weeks later, June 6, Robert Kennedy was assassinated.

It was a time of assassinations and killing young black men. Still is. I remember when Dumas got killed by that policeman. The cops claimed it was a case of mistaken identity. Some years later, the Transit Police and NYPD merged. The police claimed all records concerning the shooting were lost as a result of the merger. Surveillance were rare, and the witnesses were deemed not credible.

Well, yeah, back in them days it was nearly impossible to get any type of justice. Damn shame. And in Dumas' short life, only thirty-three years old, he had written a wealth of unpublished poetry and short stories. Toni Morrison calls him an absolute genius. When Toni was commissioning editor at Random House, she published a collection of his poetry, *Play Ebony, Play Ivory,* as well as a short story collection, *Ark of Bones.* Those collections sealed Dumas' legacy as one of the greatest, culturally insightful and politically sensitive writers of all time.

Some years later you published some of his work, right?

Yes, I did in 1988, as founding editor and publisher Literati Chicago and the Original Chicago Blues Annual, twenty years after his death. And for that opportunity, I must thank Eugene B. Redmond, Poet Laureate of East Saint Louis Illinois and executor of Henry Dumas' literary estate. Eugene was poetry editor of Literati Chicago at that time.

In 1988, Eugene B. Redmond edited a special Henry Dumas

Issue of the Black American Literature Forum, published by Indiana State University, which was a major tribute to Dumas' by several writers including Margaret Walker Alexander, Jayne Cortez, Toni Morrison, Quincy Troupe, Gwendolyn Brooks, Haki R. Madhubuti, Pinkie Gordon Lane, and many others, including me. Also, Redmond interviews Maya Angelou on Dumas; that is inspiring praise and profound insight into his writing and sensitivity.

Heavy info, Beau. Let's roll on back to '68, Boston. You covered a wide range of ladies and neighborhoods?

Always been that way. Back in the old days it could be a Winchell's doughnut and coffee for breakfast after a night of psychedelics or whatever; a greasy Polish Sausage and some beer for lunch; Dom Perignon, Poulet Cordon Bleu, and chocolate mousse for dinner, followed by a snifter of Grande Fine Champagne cognac and a smuggled Montecristo cigar. We were open to nearly everything, so there was the potential for almost anything to happen. And no matter what scene, there were ladies.

You've given a good picture of what some of your stateside swoops were like. I'm sure there is more.

Yes, much more, for a later time. I'd like to move on if we may?

Let's roll. After this last stateside romp, you went back to Québec?

Yes, I caught a ride with a rideshare from Boston to Montreal, then I hitched a ride as far as the beginning of Boulevard Laurier that becomes Grande Allee and enters Québec City. In need of another ride, I took up my hitchhiking stance. I got a ride from one of the most bizarre people I have ever met, Fred Harrower. Without exaggeration, he looked like a living drawing of a caveman. Slump, head, and a physique that indicated an extremely strong man. His car was pieced together from two different car models, a Plymouth and a Dodge. He called it a Plymouth-Dodge. The back seat was covered with tabloids like *Midnight*, *Enquirer* and several French papers. They all had pictures depicting aliens and articles about space invaders, moon men, and all kinds of other craziness. All the way into Québec City he talked about the newspapers, and how any day now the end was coming. He told me that he was worried about his wife, cats, and water coots. Water coots. I asked him what they were. He said they look a lot like cats, except they have webbed feet, and that he had twenty water coots and thirty-seven cats. He invited me to come and see them, which I did several months later. I held a water coot, and it did have webbed feet.

The drive to Québec City was about twenty minutes. Fred dropped me off, and asked if he could drop by sometimes. He also said he had never met a black person before, but that was not uncommon in certain areas of Canada. I told Gus about Fred, but he thought I was joking. About a week later, a bang on the front door, a ring of the landlady's bell, and with a shout from the street, Fred announced his presence. He stomped up the stairs, all the while talking to himself. When he entered our room, he just shouted, "Wow," then looked around. He stared at the record player and said, "You gotta tourne disque, a real tourne disque." Then he looked at eclairs on the table and shouted, "Oh boy, you've got laughing boys. Can I have one, please?" he said with the excitement of a child. And he snatched up an éclair... uh, laughing boy. It was as though he had never seen a pastry before.

The man was filthy. We could not offer him a seat. Gus looked on amazed, as I had never seen him before. I suggested we all go for a walk, and that's what we did. Once outside, Fred said he was hot and he removed his shirt. That was a sight right out of a natural history museum Neanderthal exhibit. Then he said, "I want to show you something." He stood in front of us, separated the massive amounts of hair on his chest and revealed two tits on one side of his chest and one on the other.

He had three tits? How were they located?

On the left, there were two, one underneath the other. On the right was one, but it was lower than usual. Then he said that he was sure he was from another planet, but just couldn't remember which one. Then, out of the blue he said, "I can survive quicksand. I can show you." On the same occasion that I saw the water coots, I witnessed him walking into a quicksand pit. And I need to add here that the water coots and cats were in a meshed enclosure of about 50 square feet attached to the house. I refused to go in. The place was eerily filthy.

You and Gus, now Julio I believe, had been dreaming of traveling to Africa, Europe, and beyond. You went to Europe in 1969. How did that come about?

Let me start with Gus transitioning to Julio Finn. I arrived home one day and addressed Gus as Gus, but he corrected me. He said that he was no longer Gus, but Julio Finn. Knowing how eccentric he is, that came as no surprise. He produced a small black notebook that had cursive writing faded by dampness. I could barely make out a title on the opening page. It read, "Julio's Gutter Notes, Halifax, 1958-1962." The pages that followed for the most part could not be read. Here and there I could make a sentence or just a word. Bolivia appeared on several pages as did San Francisco. Near the back was mention of Le Harve, South Hampton, and the Suez Canal. There were a few hand-drawn illustrations of would appeared to be pubs or taverns with people dancing. I asked Julio from where and from whom he had obtained the notebook. He said that he had met an old man, a stevedore and sometimes merchant seamen, at one of the bars on Boulevard Champlain frequented by those who worked the ships and docks. I love those places—they don't exist much any-more. They catered to a breed of hearty adventurers, survivors and heavy drinkers you don't see so often these days. Anyway, Gus be-came friends with the sick and aging Julio of Madagascar who asked him to keep his notebook, as he had no family. He had had other notebooks, but they had been lost. The Halifax, Nova Scotia, note-book was all he had left of his adventures, and it was badly damaged. Gus was so impressed that he decided to become Julio.

How did the name Finn come about?

Finn was the first name of the original Julio's father. Since that day, he is Julio Finn in every aspect of his life.

Now as Beau and Julio, y'all are on the move.

It was May of '69. Julio and I were on one of our sorties from Québec, having passed a long and cold winter. We decided to go Greyhound to Boston, then ride share to New York, visit friends, and call on Reverend William James. Between us we had maybe $200, courtesy of Québécois lady friends. That was chump change in New York. Well, one of the friends we were going to stay with had to leave town on an emergency, so when we gave her a call, there was

no answer, and she didn't have an answering service.
And no way she could have left you a message?
Right. But if I had had money back then, I would have hired a live telephone answering service, which was a hep way to stay in touch before answering machines became popular, and way before everyone had cell phones.

Anyway, with no place to stay, and not wanting to ask Reverend James on short notice, we checked into an Uptown dump, the Hotel Ambassador. Now let me clear here: I'm not talking about the famous Hotel Ambassador on Park Avenue and 51st. This dump Ambassador had a bar with hustler types hanging out. I met a guy at the bar, whose name I don't remember, invited me to a dice game going on upstairs in one of the rooms. Man, I had fifty dollars to my name, and Julio had less than that. But I decided to join the dice game. Take my chances. I had working a combination of luck and skill back in the old neighborhood. I was good. Sometimes that combination got me in trouble because some cats thought I was cheating. I made money on other cats' skills or lack thereof.

How did the game go, and was it a dangerous situation?
The game started out cool, but became dangerous when I started winning. For about an hour, I wasn't making nothing but side bets. I was watching other players' skills. My side bets had boosted my fifty to about two hundred. A cat asked me if I wanted to roll. I had a plan. There were five players. The average wager at the game was ten dollars with side bets around the same. I decided to up the ante. I started rolling with twenty. First roll, 11, winner. Next roll, 11, winner. Next roll with all winnings riding, plus twenty. There's a hundred from me, hundred from the guy fading me. Roll. Boom: Big Ben, or ten. The point was two fives, but I knew I could hit six-four with a long roll. You see, these guys were playing on a bed with a smooth cover. They figured there was no way a person could cheat with everybody standing around the bed keeping an eye on each other. Six-four it was, plus forty in side bets. I gots $240 including what I started with. My roll. I take money out of the game, and put up twenty. I roll for a point. It's eight, six's running mate. You got three combos to hit an eight, 6-2, 5-3, 4-4. I never go against the shooter trying to make a 6 or a 10, that's part logic, part superstition.

Anyway, I can make an eight with ease. I knew the players around the table wanted get their money back, so I offered $30 each to five players around the table. I rolled the dice, 6. I offered another $10. Now the sides bets are up to $200 and the main bet is $20. There's $220 in bets. Roll 'um, eighter from Decatur like a motherfucker! Now I gots in my pocket around $450. Cats is drinking and a friendly game was starting to shift a bit because of loser frustration. I decided to sit out for a while and let the players 'shake off their loss. That's exactly what happened over the next half hour; some of them recouped some of their losses from each other.

All right. Even though shooting craps is mostly luck, superstition, with a little skill, another element comes into play, and that is fear. When someone is on a roll, and the other guys start losing confidence, a kind of negative vibe is created, like anti-Dharma. I could see fear and worry in the faces and body language of some of the players, and I knew it was time for me to quit, or win as much as possible, as quickly as possible, then get the fuck out of that smoky room.

I re-enter the game. When my turn came, I say I want to raise the stakes to $250. The guy who should have faded me couldn't handle the bet. I offer $50 to everybody; they all were in. Roll 'um 4, could be difficult. I offer another $20. If I lose I'm damn near back where I started. But I knew they would go for the four thinking about the difficulty in making it– only two ways, 2-2, 3-1. I got $350 on the line and got to roll a four. I'm thinking of an old trick a gambler by the name of Racetrack taught me: have your opponents touch the dice because they well think that they are taking your luck of the dice and putting theirs on. "Anybody wanna touch these bones? I can't do this without you motherfuckers," I say. "Oh yeah," said one guy. "You is too lucky!" Another did the same. Now, they had touched the dice. If I lost they could revel, if I won, so be it. Roll 'um. I rolled 4-2 twice. I knew a four was coming. I let them bad boys go as I shouted, "Foe for a fine hoe!" Boom, baby, 3-1.

These cats must be getting agitated by now, right?

Understatement. Motherfuckers were mad as hell, and they had touched the dice. So, in their mind, the *hanx* was on them. Now I got $700. I'm thinking, I hope these guys don't try to take back their losses. Then a knock at the door. A well-dressed, tall, very dark and handsome young black man with a Marcel process hairdo was admitted to the den. Accolades abounded. This guy was well known in some New York street hustler circles. The gamblers called him "The Know." "Hey, Know, this young blood here is taking our money. He ain't cheating, but he a lucky motherfucker," exclaimed the guy who brought me into the game. I said that I was just lucky. Know said to me, "Come on man, uh what's your name?" I thought about my answer and said, "Jenkins." The Know said I didn't look like no Jenkins, and that didn't matter anyway, he was there to win money—mine and everybody else's. I was real low key, didn't want to offend him in any way, because I didn't want to get shot or stabbed. And I'm sure I looked like a square to these guys with my un-ironed blue dress shirt, paisley tie, jeans, sport coat, old style combat boots, and completely wild hair. The Know looked at me and was trying hard not to crack up. I'm sure he was thinking something like, *These chumps let this square-ass motherfucker take their money.*

Now, there are six of you in this hotel room with a bed, and the usual things like a TV and a table.

Right. It wasn't so large, maybe comfortable for two people. Everybody stood or sat around the bed while shooting dice. The shooter stood at the foot of the bed and rolled the dice toward the head.

Is there drinking, and other things going on?

Yeah. Drinking and a lot more. Basically, they were doing everything except shooting up. Somebody was sharing a fifth of whiskey. Somebody else was offering pills, asking if you wanna go up or down. The Know passed a joint around. I took a hit to be cordial, but I didn't want anything to mess up my concentration; also, he seemed like the type of guy that would be offended if I had refused. And they all smoked cigarettes, as did I at that time.

The Know. He wants to show the other cats that he can break your streak. What happened next?

The Know entered the game. He had the dice first. He rolled for $40, and was faded by the guy who invited me. His point was six, and he made on the second roll. The guy that brought me dropped out of the game. He did not have a good night and may have lost most of his money. It was my turn to fade. Okay, $40. The Know's point is nine. I drop a hundred on the table. "You ain't gone nine,' I say. I'm trying to scare The Know, make him unsure. Well, he reached in his pocket and out with a Cincinnati bankroll. Five-hundred-dollar bill on the outside and about three inches of other denominations tucked inside. He said, "Don't stop with a hundred. You want some of this... come on," Okay. I've got $240 in the game now. I'm hoping he can't make it. The Know rolls. I call the dice before they stop. That's one of the rules in street craps. You can stop the roll by saying, "I got these!" Good thing, because he rolled 6-3. Man, was he pissed. He rolled again. 3-2. I didn't say anything, but I realized he didn't know how to re-roll that first nine. I knew he was gonna lose because he didn't flip that die that showed 2. I decided to go for more. I dropped another hundred. High cats in the background are saying shit like, "Damn!" Gone be some shit up in the motherfucker this evening y'all." They went on and on, contributing to the excitement and tension. Now I've got $340 in the game. The Know rattles and shakes the dice. He calls upon Nina Ross, the goddess of nines. He's too fucking tense, man. He rolls, shouts, "Yeah, for my black ass, baby." The dice stop. Seven. Very casually, I take my money. I now have around $1,000 in my pocket, and I'm watching the characters in the room. I had already thought about how to take three of them out if they tried something.

Damn Beau, your ass was just as dangerous and crazy as these guys.

Right. If they started some shit I know, at the very least, one of them motherfuckers was gonna be hurting real bad.

What happened next?

I didn't want my luck to run out, and I didn't want to get greedy and lose everything. And at the same time, The Know was embarrassed and determined to get his money back. I suggested that we roll the dice three times for $1,000. Not $1,000 per roll, but the best of three, and no matter how it goes, we'll agree to call it an evening. I also wanted the other cats to leave, go downstairs and out of the hotel so we could see them from the room window. I thought The Know would disagree, but instead he suggested to the others that they should leave. And they did. Maybe some sensed trouble and were glad to leave, while the others seemed indifferent.

Now, it's just us two. We rolled to see who would go first. The Know won the roll. I stopped his first roll six times. None were winners. Then he rolled snake eyes. One down. My turn. I rolled eleven. Game over. The Know turned out to be a gentleman without the others around. I took the money from the bed. I had just over $2,000 in my pocket. The Know probably had another grand in his pocket, but a deal is a deal. We left together and agreed not to talk about the outcome. I didn't. I had a drink at the bar and disappeared to our hotel room, where I found Julio half sleep in a chair with *Amos and Andy* blasting on the TV.

I entered the room and said to Julio, loudly, "Wake you Black, Negro ass up!" "Huh." "Wake up motherfucker, we going to leave this motherfucker, tomorrow." I put cool to the side and was dancing around the room. Then I showed him the cash. He couldn't believe it. And so it was the dice game that changed and redirected our lives. The crap shoot that opened the gates of Africa, Europe, Asia ... the world. The crap shoot that opened the door to romance, adventure, great and sometimes painful learning experiences. And you know, since then I've played craps maybe twice, and not at all in the last thirty years, but I have won nicely at the Boule tables in Cassis, Nice, and Monte Carlo. More on that later.

You've got money. What was the next move?

LaBosse, we were too excited to sleep. This was the game-changer we'd been dreaming about since we were fourteen, fifteen years old. We used to walk down State Street in Chicago and stare at the offerings in the TWA office, the Pan Am office, Iberia, Air France, and all the others, and just dream. I was especially fascinated by BOAC, British Overseas Airways Corporation, because they had some really sharp planes called VC10 and they flew to many destinations in Africa. Unfortunately for the Africans, these destinations were former colonies that had been well thrashed by the British Empire. But we still wanted to be around black people in a black land.

We left the hotel at seven in the morning with shopping and plane tickets on our minds. Back in 1969, two thousand dollars went a long way. First stop, Brooks Brothers, where Julio and I bought straw hats and classic Brooks Brothers dress shirts without a button-down collar, which was too Ivy. Then on to Rogers Peet at 42nd and Fifth Avenue, where I bought a gray, three piece, all-season suit for $150. Julio decided to hold off on a suit until we got to London. By 10am we had tickets in hand. We found one-way tickets to London on BOAC for around $250.

Your money is already dwindling. Did you still feel the excitement?

Oh yes. One thing about money is that if you have some, it's easier to get more. So we weren't worried. In fact, I had a line of credit with a good friend, Fran, who I had paid back about a year earlier. She was really a supporter of the arts and admired me for my determination to become a writer and professional musician. In her past she had been a violinist with the Boston Symphony; she was now composing. She lived in New York City with her husband of twenty years who was not particularly fond of me, or any black people. But that's an old story, unworthy of repetition. I gave Fran a call and luckily she was home. I told her the whole story which I knew she would find fascinating– that's the kind of woman she was. I told her I had around $1,300 left and needed a bit more money in order to arrive in Europe with a little reserve. Fran insisted that she come by the hotel and give us a lift to JFK. She picked us up around one o'clock, in her pearl white Jaguar XJ 6, and drove us to Kennedy to make a four o'clock flight to London. While unloading the car curbside, Fran passed me an envelope and said, "Sweetheart, this is not a loan. This is a small investment in your great future. To know that you are well is the only dividend I'm interested in. I love you, but may not be able to see you again." Before I could say anything, she kissed me. "Shush," said Fran. "Call me collect when you can." She left. Julio and I headed to the check-in.

What a stellar woman. What a loving and fitting departure. What were you feeling as you were about to board, about to exit the U.S.A., friends, and family?

Everything felt good. There were absolutely no feelings of regret, or feeling like I was leaving some things or some persons I would miss. The only thing I wanted was to get on the plane, feel the surge of the takeoff, and have a drink.

Back in those days, getting on a plane was not terribly dif-

ferent from queuing up to get on a bus or train. You just got on according to seating order. No security. No ignorant-ass motherfuckers trying to bring airplanes down.
I can dig that.
　Yeah man, after all the announcements and free drinks, the take-off. I felt like a two-thousand-pound cyclops just fell off my back.
How was your flight—exciting?
　Themost exciting moment on the flight was when I went to the restroom and opened the envelope from Fran. Boom! Fifteen hundred dollars. I let a scream. A moment later there was a knock on the bathroom door from a stewardess asking if everything was okay. I said, "Yeahhhh. Baby, I'm fine just fine." Then I opened the door and peeped out and said to her, "You wanna come in? Just kidding, thanks for asking." She laughed, but almost in an interested kind of way. Her eyes said a lot, kind of an *if I could I would* look, then she walked away, turned around and smiled.
You know you wrong!
　Yeah, I know. I was just kidding though. But had she been able to come on in under different circumstances, I think she may have. We got friendly during the flight. She passed me her phone number in London, as I told her we would looking for a flat, and she thought maybe she could help. Vera was her name. Unfortunately, I never saw her again after the flight, and eventually I lost her phone number. Pretty young lady. Early twenties. Redhead. Vera.
　We arrived at Heathrow the following morning, having slept very little and still slightly tipsy. We were concerned about Customs and Immigration Control since we were traveling with one-way tickets. We had heard from others that if you didn't have a round-trip ticket or lots of cash, you could be sent back to wherever you came from. Not a problem. My Rogers Peet suit did the trick. When asked how long I would be in the U.K., my answer was that I would be departing to Addis Ababa in a few days and was in the process of finalizing travel plans with colleagues in the U.K. That was good enough for the Immigration Officer. I was in. Julio concocted a statement equally as false, and he was in. Only then, at that moment of being admitted to England, did I feel real joy and relief being out of

the United States.

You had no second thoughts?

None whatsoever after my parents' stories, along with those of other black people of their generation. After assassinations, riots, blatant and institutionalized racism, my own experiences, the Vietnam War, and more—man, I was so happy to be someplace else.

Did you think Europe would be different?

I thought there would be a style difference. How prejudice is manifested would not be as aggressive. I never had any illusions about Europeans. I mean they are America's mother. Americans got their fucked-up ideas from Europe. Think about it. Slavery, Puritanism, Christianity, White supremacy, genocide– all of that comes from Europeans. But the bigger difference is that throughout Europe's turmoil and troubles, there have been thinkers and intellectuals who vehemently opposed the status quo. The result is that once Europeans make a correction, they go all out to reinvent themselves. Look at post-Nazi Germany and the laws they set into place themselves. Or the work of the English Abolitionist Movement, advanced by enlightened thinkers as early as the beginning of the 1700s. The United States had and has a long way to go. Like in South Africa, old demons don't just roll over and die. You have to capture them, run them out and hopefully not have killing conflicts, the way they've killed. The idea is peaceful coexistence, and to be a better person than those who took so much from your people for so long. We felt that we could have a life without the constant threat of violence and discrimination. Many others, black writers, musicians, artists, retired military, have made their homes throughout Europe, finding enough tranquility and appreciation for their work to be able to live and create in peace.

Now y'all are in and feeling good. What happened next?

We knew England had a love affair with the Blues, and that Great Bluesmen, like Sonny Boy Williamson, had been treated well by the Yardbirds, John Mayall, and others. The Rolling Stones got a direct infusion of Electric Blues from Muddy Waters. We knew about some hep record stores around Shaftesbury, and the 100 Club on Oxford Street. Going for what we knew, we hopped into a black cab and asked the driver to recommend a cheap hotel near the music action. We had no idea where we were going, but we ended up at a spot, a kind of bed and breakfast, not far from Leicester Square.

Were you too excited to flop?

We were. We couldn't wait to hit the streets. You can imagine what it was like to experience all new things like fashion, language, and money. These were the days of Guineas, Pounds, Shillings and Pence. It took a while to figure that out. I don't recall feeling cheated with the money, not like in France when a shop keeper gave me change for a fifty Franc note in Old Francs. Worthless.

Well, we walked and walked. Piccadilly, Oxford Circus, Trafalgar Square, on and on. We walked to the popular Carnaby Street, where fashion designers had shops, and the Mod and hep dressers would stroll along. Julio bought a suit from a shop. I wasn't with him; I was too tired so I relaxed in a cafe. Man, that suit was laughable. It was the worst fitting thing I had ever seen on him. Now, the man is slim, as you know. I think he couldn't find anything cut narrow and long enough. What he bought was hanging off of him, and the bell-bottom pants were too short and flooded, exposing his hiking boots. He thought he was sharp, but to me he looked like one of those cats who when they get out of jail, they give them an ill-fitting suit to start a new life.

Did you ridicule him?

Hell, yes. I said, "How can you waste my hard-earned gambling winnings on that ugly-ass suit with highwater pants?" You know him—he thinks he is right until proven wrong. So, after moving around a bit more and he could see what the real hep dressers were wearing, he stopped wearing the pants and wore the suit coat as a sport coat with some nice-looking jeans. Later, in Paris, after we started making money, he ceremoniously burned that ugly suit. And over the years he became known as one of the best-dressed men in Paris. He wore suits from Old England and had several custom made by reputable tailors.

By now, after all the walking, you must have been wiped out?

We walked back to the hotel and crashed. We needed to. We had been rolling for hours and hours. We'd been excited for over forty-eight hours. Finally, no more. Time to sleep.

Next day?

The next day Julio got in touch with his brother, Jerome Arnold, who was living in London. Jerome was living near Shepherds Bush with his lady, Jan. He knew London well and was having meetings with John Lennon about some project. I never found out what happened with that, but Jerome has always been working on projects. And in those days, he hadn't been gone too long from the Paul Butterfield Blues Band. We had a great evening with Jerome who was full of advice, especially about not spending money—which was just the opposite of how I was thinking. Jerome had a thing about being thrifty. I think he was over-the-top with his thrift obsession, to the point of not being able to enjoy his fame and the possibilities that can go along with it. I didn't see Jerome again until 1974, when I lived with him for a few months on Lundys Lane in San Francisco. Those were great days, and I'll get to them later.

Okay. So, you got around the West End of London. Shopped. Visited Jerome, record stores. I know London was cheaper then, but still, even with the money from Fran, your money had to be running short. What was your next move?

The money was thinning. We decided to spend the summer in Amsterdam and go there via Paris. The next day we checked out of the hotel and took a flight to Paris. We arrived in the afternoon and immediately got a taxi. The destination: Place de Clichy. The reason: Henry Miller's book, *Quiet Days in Clichy*. The outcome: disappointment.

Disappointment?

Yes, in terms of being young and not thinking clearly, we struck out. Henry Miller wrote his book in 1956 about his days in living near Place de Clichy in 1934. At that time, between wars, there was a flourishing of artists, writers, poets, and philosophers, all gathering constantly in Montmartre. The Place Clichy Miller wrote about, specifically the Cafe Wepler, had completely changed. Gone were the prostitutes and artists. There were no indecent acts taking place under the tables. There was no music. It was bland and boring. But now things have changed. The cafe is embracing its one hundred-plus years tradition of being a major player in the lives of artists and writers. They even sponsor a literary prize. When we arrived in 1969, it was before the Cafe Wepler transitioned into a new era. I guess we arrived between eras, and that represented around twenty-five years. I asked a waiter about Henry Miller but he was clueless. Now the staff knows the history, and thanks to the internet, so do many others.

You hadn't checked into a hotel yet?

No man, that's how eager and excited we were. We were at the cafe with our bags. We were a sight to see. Bags, suits, straw hats, drinking wine, and asking our waiter about the past. He knew nothing, and he had probably been working there twenty years or more, all during the Cafe Wepler in-between time.

Where did you go after the Cafe Wepler?

Next on our places to go list was the *Rive Gauche, Quartier Latin.* But we lowered our expectations after the Wepler disappointment. We arrived by taxi in Place Sainte-Michel *jusqu en face de la rue de la Huchette.* Man, Place Sainte-Michel was jumping. Cafes, discotheques, biblioteques, people mingling, street artists, and the greyish-brown buildings of Paris. There is something romantic in that greyness, something familiar to me, even though I had not previously set eyes upon those buildings.

We walked the Place with amazement and enthusiasm, not knowing or caring where we were going. However, there was a significant police presence. The CRS, Compagnies Républicaines de Sécurité, also known as riot police, had buses loaded with troops, and those walking about the Place had shields and helmets. You know, riot gear. They looked fierce. I had been fighting police in some way in Chicago on and off as a teenager, but I had never seen riot police just walking among the people. I'd seen them chasing people, and me getting chased. But we knew that this was not atypical in some European countries during that time, even though their history is full of protests, wars, revolutions, enforcement, and radical changes.

Was there a specific reason for the CRS presence in this area?

Yes. We were told by a Dutch couple in the Cafe Sainte-Michel that it was the anniversary of the May 1968 student protests and worker strikes that, for a bit, set France on its ass. Even the President, Charles de Gaulle, temporarily left the country. At one point, there were eleven million workers on strike, and protesting. What police force can contain that many of their fellow citizens? Shit, if you lose your people, kill, and imprison them, you don't have a country– only ignorant, angry, and violent flunky-ass police and politicians.

Did anything happen that evening?

Fortunately, no. But a short time later I got caught in the middle of riots in Paris and Amsterdam.

In Paris, I made it into a cafe just before the riot squad attacked. In Amsterdam, I was just walking down the street and I heard a distant roar that grew louder and louder. I turned a corner, and damn, there were hundreds of people running towards me being attacked by police on horseback. I turned and ran my ass off, as did other people. I was running down a canal street when a policeman on horseback starting closing in. He was right on top of me with his club raised. I said to him, "Hey, I'm not in this. I'm trying to get home." He didn't give a fuck. He paused for a moment then tried to hit me. He missed. I got out of the way. He raised the club again while trying to control his horse. This time my basketball jumping skills helped me. I shocked him. I jumped up, snatched him off his horse, and slam-dunked his ass to the ground. Cheers erupted. I fled like a 100-yard dash sprinter, pushed one slow-ass protesting guy into the canal. I didn't have nothing to protest about. I had to push people out of my way. I finally made it back to where I was staying on Roemer Visscherstraat.

What happened to the person in the canal?

His friends pulled him out. It was written about in the newspaper the next day– the entire protest was.

And the cop?

I don't know what happened to that motherfucker. I'd imagine that he got back on his horse and kept on trying to beat people. You know, I was concerned about walking around town after that, concerned about the police. But nothing happened.

No riots that night in Paris, thankfully. I know the CRS, Gendarme– none of them cops mess around. Had you yanked one of them off his horse you may have been in big trouble and seriously injured.

No doubt. I was lucky in Amsterdam. The real drag was being caught up in somebody else's politics and grievances.
What did you do for a hotel?
We chatted with the Dutch couple for awhile. They recommended that we take a walk down Rue de la Harpe, where there were some not-so-pricey hotels.

We found a hotel, checked in, freshened up, and began roaming. We came across a jazz bar called Storyville on Rue de la Huchette, near the corner of Rue Petit Pont. It was one dim and smoky long and narrow room with a bar nearly the length of the room. There was a narrow space for walking back and forth to the restrooms, and just enough room for small tables alongside the wall opposite the bar and near the front door. The walls had photos of jazz and blues greats. The air was filled with music being played through a top-of-the-line Grundig sound system. The area behind the bar had several racks of LP's. Nearly everybody in jazz and blues was represented. Storyville was a jazz lover's Utopia.

Behind the bar this particular evening was Jacques Bisceglia: bar manager, photographer, brawler, detective story enthusiast. One of the first things he said to me was, "I'm not afraid of you. I'll fight you if you want." At first I thought he was nuts. Then the old truth I had previously learned occurred to me. Some white men have a thing about fighting black men. A kind of Jim Jefferies syndrome. Jefferies wanted to win the heavyweight boxing title from Jack Johnson for the White race. Insanity. Who gives a fuck. But Jacques was trapped in foolishness by his testosterone, ego, and racism. He felt threatened by black men, but immersed himself in black culture at the same time. I told him I had no interest in fighting him, but if he messed with me, I'd figure out a way to fuck him up, either during the fight or afterward– even years later. He thought about what I was saying and backed off. About thirty years later Jacques and I met near his collectible book and photograph stall along the Seine. Both of us having matured, we had a civil conversation about those times and how we had changed over the years.   He contributed compelling photographs to my book, *Great Black Music,* about the Art Ensemble of Chicago. In 1998 during an Art Ensemble tour I gave him a copy of the book hot off the press. Regrettably, that was the last time I saw him. He passed away in March of 2013 at age 72. Jacques published a book of stunning photography called *Black and White Fantasy* that should be checked out by anyone that loves jazz-life images.

You know when Muhammad Ali became heavyweight champion, and then a Muslim, white boys were often looking to fight. Even back in high school, punk-ass Irish wannabe brawlers wanted to fight. By fighting a Black, they got to vent their hatred for Ali and black people in general. If they won a fight, I bet their dicks stayed hard for a month. Sick-ass motherfuckers, I'm telling you!

Was there anybody in the bar who overheard your conversation?

Yes. Seated near down the bar a bit from our conversation was Claude Delcloo, a *JazzMagazine* editor, drummer, record producer who was about to impact the lives of nearly every jazz musician who came to Paris for the next couple of years with recordings and concerts. And unbeknownst to us all back then, those projects would survive the test of time and become a major chapter in the black music continuum. Delcloo was producer for the legendary BYG Actuel record label.

Claude and Jacques knew each other?

Oh, yeah. Jacques was the main photographer for the label, and he was also very instrumental in finding talent. Many people thought he was a partner in BYG because the name is comprised of the surnames of the owners: Fernand Baruso, Jean-Luc Young, and Jean Georgakarakos, and Jacques' surname was Bisceglia.

Well, this was our first meeting with Claude, who didn't hesitate to introduce himself and tell us about his project. He intended to record every free jazz or avant-garde artist in the world. He had admirable, huge ambitions. Julio and I said we were blues performers and blues poets. Claude immediately imagined blues,-free jazz-poetry amalgamations. He told us about the Pan-African Festival in Algeria, put on by the Organization for African Unity, coming up in July, and that he couldn't invite us because all the money was budgeted, but we could come if we wanted and BYG would pay the hotel. Maybe, we said, and would let him know.

Did you go to Algeria?

No. For one thing we were nearly out of money, no idea from where more was coming. And since our plan was to head to Ams-

terdam, we needed to hang on to the little money that remained.
And Delcloo?

Delcloo said many recording sessions would take place after Algeria from August onward, and that the Paris music scene would be jumping like never before. He offered me a recording deal without hearing a note. Of course, I agreed. The drawback was that there would be no upfront money until nearer the session date, which would be in the fall. The massing of musicians in Paris would take place after Algeria.

You headed to Amsterdam?

We took the train from Gare du Nord right into Amsterdam Centraal. We had heard that it is extremely difficult to find an apartment in Amsterdam, but we got lucky. Just near the train station was a public message board attached to an information kiosk. I immediately saw a small, hand-printed sign for an apartment to rent. I took down the notice and several others with the same offer. I called, and within an hour we were sitting in the living room of Hank Tielmann, on the Westerstraat. We loved his apartment, which consisted of five rooms plus kitchen and bath. This was an extraordinary find. This apartment was huge by most European standards. Tielmann was going on holiday in the U.S. for two months and wanted to rent it out during his absence. We negotiated the price to within about 100 Guilders of our remaining money, and paid him for the entire two months. But there was a catch: he wasn't leaving for two weeks. This meant we had to find a place to stay, and we had no money.

No money. Did you know anyone?

No, but it was certainly time to meet somebody. Sometimes there's nothing worse than being near broke. Why not just be totally broke? With those thoughts as inspiration, we walked to a rather large populated cafe near Rembrandtplein and immediately ordered a bottle of Dutch wine. Half the money gone. The young, twenty-ish waiter, Brecht, was curious as to where we came from since we were not speaking Dutch, Tango, or Kwinti like black people from the former Dutch colony of Surinam, an island nation in the Caribbean. When we told him we were Chicago Bluesman, we immediately had a friend and fan. We told Brecht our story. Brecht, as it turned out, had several contacts, including a former schoolmate that lived in a residence for pious Catholic young men that embraced a strict moral code including the exclusion of female company. No surprise there. Brecht suggested that he contact his friend and see if there was availability at the residence. He called, explained our situation to his friend, who in turn explained it to the director. After about an hour, the director, Desmond Sweeney, called Brecht at the cafe and said we should come by right away as it was getting late and evening prayers would begin soon.

Brecht explained that even though this was not a situation tailor-made for a couple of young Bluesmen, we may be able to sleep there if we maintained a low profile and were not disruptive. His friend had run out of money, couldn't find a job, and because of his family's connections with the Church, he was able to stay there until his condition improved.

What happened when you arrived?

Sweeney welcomed us into a reception area that was appointed like a living room—chairs, coffee table with religious magazines. There were religious paintings and prints on the walls depicting saints and angels with animals and birds looking mindless. There were also photographs of past popes, some who looked pop-eyed as though something was stuck up their ass, while others looked severe and stern. The large picture of the then current pope, Paul VI, that had really dark eyeballs. I later learned those eyeballs were peep holes.

Peep holes! That's consistent with the thinking of zealots, censors, and witch hunters. There may have been more peep-holes around there than you found out about.

I wouldn't be surprised. Those people were obsessed with control. Sweeney conducted an interview that centered around morals and eventually, how we were going to pay. We explained our situation, finding an apartment that would be ready in two weeks and we embellished the amount of pending wire transfers from zero to a few hundred dollars. He took our passports for the required police check, then led us to our new temporary home in the basement. It was a single room with three narrow beds, each against a wall that bore nauseatingly gruesome portrayals of scenes from the Bible, angels, saints, and who knows who. They all had halos, bleeding hearts, and characterless or tormented faces. There was a closet, a large table in the center of the room, and a sofa. The room had two entrances, one from the hall that led to the dining room that was also in the basement, and another that opened onto a garden, that was shared by other properties that I later discovered were once occupied by nuns.

What was the day-to-day life like?

For us it was boring. Breakfast together was mandatory, and it was served around seven in the morning. However, one could be excused if they had to work. Most of the other 20 residents attended breakfast.

In the beginning, all were curious about us, and most had never met a black person before. The questions ranged from naive to downright racist. How does it feel to be a Negro? Can you dance? Do you love Christ? Are Negro girls as shameless and loose as we've heard? And on and on. To the Negro girls question, I responded that it is Europeans who have been the White-conquering, mega-worm, forcing themselves sexually upon women, men, and children wherever they planted their flag, and that lie about women of color is nothing more than Euro-Christian hypocrisy and victim blaming. The rest of their questions did not merit much more than polite dismissal.

I know they didn't like hearing that.

No, they did not. That subject was never mentioned again. And you know, sometimes it's hard to determine if people who ask such questions are stupid or naïve, or if they think you are.

It's probably a combination. Did you make friends with any of them?

One young man seemed a bit different from the others. He was French, and his name was Jean. We called him Frenchy, which reflects our thinking at the time. He liked being called that though. Frenchy was an expert at thwarting Sweeney's code of conduct, and he showed us the ropes of living in a pious, male Catholic community. He showed us how to sneak and out and back in at night by jimmying the locks, as Sweeney had an eleven o'clock curfew. Unbelievable. The oldest guy in the place was forty or so, and he was compliantly bringing his ass home by curfew. Of course, there were exceptions, but each case was decided by Sweeney. I was perplexed by the behavior of grown men. Something was just too strange about this "residence for men," so I asked Frenchy if these guys were in some sort of secret society. Frenchy said the place was operated by Opus Dei, a rather secretive ultra-religious organization, with an extremely strict and conservative practice of Catholicism. They banned books, films, music, culture, sex, etcetera, and some of them whipped themselves. Damn! I thought to myself. These some crazy-ass white people. I asked Frenchy what the fuck was he doing there. Family, he said. He was trying to please his family. I told Frenchy that when we moved into our new place he would begin his march to freedom.

Opus Dei. You didn't know that when he rented you the room.

He never mentioned it. He only said the name of the house, *Liedenhoven.* And we never let on that we knew. And funny, not a motherfucker in there said a word about Opus Dei.

It must have been a real test of your wills to be at Sweeney's for those two weeks.

Indeed it was, but Frenchy was a beacon, a real godsend. He knew a few sex-workers over in the Red Light District where he often visited during his clandestine sorties. He said he never had sexual encounters, he just enjoyed their company. He introduced us around the district to cafe people, shop owners, and ladies. I became friends with Kitty, an absolutely beautiful and spirited Sinti woman. Kitty. She was right out of the song by the Impressions, "Gypsy Woman." I mean, from head to toe, fine. Her breath could have been a scent from heaven. Dark, dark hair, eyes. Her skin was the hue of Ethiopian opal. She was thirty years old when we met. We remained friends for years, until she married and left Holland. She was an extraordinary human being in so many ways: she danced, played violin, and could sing me into hypnosis. I often think about her and hope that her life has gone well.

What else happened to help you through your time at Sweeney's?

I mentioned earlier that I had been caught up in the middle of riots in Amsterdam. I walked around concerned that I could be arrested for snatching that policeman off his horse. That never happened. We passed the time sleeping, relaxing in cafes, and occasionally going to hear music at Paradiso, the famous music hall that was a converted theater, much like Bill Graham's Fillmore in San Francisco and Fillmore East in New York. We continued sneaking out at night, and eventually, Julio managed to sneak a young lady in and out. That night was big fun as we were all drunk, laughing, and stumbling around trying not to wake up Sweeney, or worse, the nervous Spaniard, Carlos. Carlos was Sweeney's right-hand man and self-appointed enforcer.

How much longer could you take being at the Residence?

Not much longer. On Thursday, June 19, two days ahead of schedule, we moved into our apartment at Westerstraat 125 and immediately commenced a summer of decadence, tempered with self-imposed time for reading and writing. We didn't want to lose sight of our goal to become writers.

Oh, of course not. But you were how old?

I was twenty and Julio twenty-one. The discipline didn't come easily. Then again, one of the advantages of youth is the ability to bounce back quickly from serious partying. We didn't fall too far out of step. If my memory serves me, we decided to pass an entire week immersed in some intellectual pursuit. I wrapped my head around Perez Galdos, Richard Wright, Herman Hesse, and the Marquis de Sade. And at the end of that disciplined period, I locked myself in my room with a bottle of Dutch brandy, champagne, and Kitty. Kitty...have mercy!

I know you did something wild to initiate the apartment. What was it?

Outside of our declared week of intellectual stimulation, nearly every moment of every day was dedicated to hedonism, or recovering from it. The same day that we moved into our apartment, friends arrived from several cities and became house guests. Ellie and Jenna from Boston; Angelique from Haiti; Micheline from Montreal, who once declared herself the leading white slut on earth; and longtime friend Greece from Chicago. And there were local people that we had met who dropped by: Brecht the waiter; LaBron C. Prater, trumpeter, and the bevy of Dutch babes he seemed to always have with him. So, the first night was a kind of house warming that wasn't wild at all. We had lots of laughs about Sweeney and Carlos and our evening sneak-outs. Leaving Sweeney's was like having shackles removed. Freedom, finally.

A house full of guests, and freedom finally, then what?

Julio came up with a novel idea. He called it newspaper poetry, which was a lot like a Tweet today, only published in a newspaper. Just a few characters to express a thought. He came up with inviting the world to dinner in order for us to let the world know we were in Amsterdam. Julio and I went to the Want Ads office of De-Telegraaf and placed the ad which read nearly as follows:

Who would invite the world to dinner? We would.
Ellie Sennewald, Julio Finn, Lincoln T. Beauchamp, LaBron Prater, Maurice Oliver.
June 29, 1969, Westerstraat 128, Amsterdam, 17,00h.

Julio was thinking big. Invite the world?

Ah, yes. We all had the idea... the world is ours! And why not? People reach out globally in huge numbers today. Look at Facebook, Uber, others. We didn't know if anyone would even show, but everybody on the planet was invited.

The world's been invited. What's next?

Preparations. We had about $500 between us to feed the world. We decided that spaghetti and meat sauce would have to do, along with as much wine as we could afford. We bought four huge, approximately 20-liter pots: three for cooking pasta and one for the sauce. I was the cook. Twenty kilos of ground pork and beef, tomatoes, garlic, spices, pepperoncini, Parmesan cheese, wine. Boom. The meat sauce was happening. I mixed the sauce and pasta into three pots, which were huge vats. We had bottles of wine throughout the apartment along with glasses, plastic cups, tea cups, and anything else that could hold liquid. We had stacks of plastic plates and rolls of paper towels throughout. The idea was not to be elegant or serve multiple courses; it was to feed as many people as we could, as they marveled at the whole idea.

What kind of people came?

Here's how it went. We blocked the downstairs door open at 6 o'clock; no need to ring the bell. We lived on the top floor, the third floor, so we could hear the early visitors coming up the creaky staircase which ended at our front door that was wide open. In the first hour about twenty people came. They sat around and of course wanted to know just what was happening. How and why would someone invite the world to dinner? They were also somewhat surprised to see that the hosts were four young people: three handsome black men, and an attractive white woman, all from the United States. Man, there were all kinds of reactions and interpretations. One guy was sure that we were CIA on a mission to explore Dutch personalities. I couldn't convince him otherwise, so I told him to think as he wishes. He left early in the evening, then returned with three other fellows that he claimed were BVD, the Dutch secret service. I pissed him off. I told him I know BVD, it's an underwear company in the U.S., and it stands for Better Value in Drawz. He didn't think that was funny after I explained what "drawz" are and suggested that he and his boys could be skid marks. I told him that he was taking an evening of fun too seriously. We had no hidden agendas. I invited him and his BVD boys to leave, and they did. And this is a thing that might happen at any kind of open gathering: you don't know who may show up.

Any other people stand out?

There was a most interesting, frail looking Dutchman of about fifty years old and assisted by a cane, who came with his son. His son led him through the apartment. He looked around intensely, while occasionally focusing his stare at a particular individual for no apparent reason. He looked at people dancing, eating, smoking, laughing with such a stare that I felt the need to ask if he was okay. He said he was fine. I had asked people sitting on a sofa to slide over so that he and his son could sit. I pulled up a chair, sat in front of them, and introduced myself. They in turn introduced themselves. They were both Hans, father and son. The elder Hans explained that he had not been off his property since the end of World War Two in 1945 because he was completely disillusioned with war-like Europe, and the cruel world generally. When he read our ad inviting the world to dinner he decided that he would accept the invitation just to see who would extend such an invitation, and who might show up. His son explained a little about his war past, and that he was a recent widower. Injuries, Nazi occupation, his participation in the Dutch Resistance, all played a role in his isolation. I introduced him to the other hosts, and really, the stories he told would make a film or volumes of memories. Amazing man. And because of coming to our home and enjoying himself, he told us that his days of isolation were over. In the weeks that followed, he dropped by to say hello from time to time. He was always welcomed.

I wish I had been there. What about the seriousness of Hans' visit amidst all the partying?

Totally positive. Invite the world and you're going to get worldly stories, hopefully. Another thing that happened was that the press showed up. A lady from a newspaper came to check us out. By the time she arrived, which was around 9 o'clock, the party was in full swing. Many people had brought liquor, wine, marijuana, and hashish... you know. The joint was rocking, the building was rocking, the nearby canals were rocking. There was no way the press was going to get an interview. The newspaper lady, Annemieke, agreed to return the following evening when things were more quiet. She snapped a few pictures, but she wasn't expecting what she saw; if she had, she would have brought a regular photographer. There were around a hundred people inside the apartment and dozens along the stairway and street waiting to get in.

There was no room to move around in the apartment. Some people had coupled off, tripled off, and more and were doing things huddled on the floor in closets and hanging out on the beds and in the bathroom. I had to stay sober to remain in control. Around 11 o'clock, after the food and wine we had bought were long gone, the crowd starting thinning. And right at 11:30, Frenchy squeezed himself into the apartment. He had waited until after the Sweeney nightcheck to sneak out.

I'm sure he was happy to be on the scene, get them shackles off.

LaBosse, let me tell you, Frenchy didn't waste any time with the ladies. He met Suzette, a beautiful young woman maybe 23, 24 years old. I mean stunning, statuesque, ebony, light brown eyes. She was from Surinam. Her mother was from Martinique, and her father was Surinamese. Her parents met as they were both working in The Hague. That's what I found out about her in a brief conversation. She had come with a Dutch guy, but he left when she showed interest in Frenchy. And Frenchy was styling that night. He was the only person to show up in a suit. He had that Ted Lapidus look, you remember? Double breasted jacket, slightly flared trousers, white shirt with buttons opened halfway down the chest, and some hep shoes, like Bruno Magli. So Frenchy came to deal with the ladies, and deal he did. He also brought several bottles champagne to *boire tot le matin avec des amis*. I stashed them in the forbidden sanctum where no one was allowed, a WC cubicle off the kitchen.

Around 2 in the morning, I had successfully gotten our remaining guests to leave. There were around 10 people left besides us hosts. They were either there at our request, as were Frenchy and Suzette, and a couple of others, or they were too fucked up to leave. They had passed out.

Were people respectful of your house, nothing damaged or missing?

They were very respectful and careful. As a result, the cleanup was accomplished with ease. A funny thing happened around 10 in the morning as I was just starting to move around, make some coffee, and begin restoring order. Now, check out the scene. Frenchy and Suzette had passed out on the largest sofa in the living room. Suzette's half-naked ass was Frenchy's pillow. I remember when they fell asleep over there and her ass was in her panties even though her skirt was slightly up. Now, Frenchy's face was buried in her crack, snoring. They were both snoring.

I know you. I'm sure you would not have minded being in Frenchy's place?

You know that's right. Suzette...toss her salad for days! Anyway, I got two pots of filtered coffee going and washed out some cups and glasses, as some of those invited to stay were starting to move around. After a while, having had coffee, three of them thanked us profusely for our hospitality and a good time, then headed downstairs to the streets. I put the champagne in the refrigerator and continued to clean. At this point only Ellie, Lebron, Julio, Greece, Frenchy, Suzette, Jenna, Angelique, Micheline, and I were left in the flat. People were sleeping on sofas and on the beds and in huge chairs. And succumbing to a wave of exhaustion, I slumped into a huge older, brocaded living room chair with an ottoman. I glanced over at Frenchy and Suzette, raised my eyebrows, then passed out.

Seems like a peaceful and pleasant end to what had been a

successful and fun evening.

Ah, yeah. It was fun and was to become more fun and funny. Just as I was passing out in that chair, there came a rapping at the door. Five rapid hard knockings, followed by five more, bap-bap-bap-bap-bap. I thought it was the police or maybe someone forgot something. I shouted for whoever to come on in– the door's open. Enter Sweeney. This motherfucker's eyeballs popped out so far that they damn near stuck to the lenses of his glasses. His mouth fell open. And his Celtic pale face became alabaster, then reddened as though he just drank a triple shot of Jameson' chased by a pint of Guinness. Ellie and Jenna were on a sofa in bra and panties with a sheet draped over them, but not covering them completely. Julio was passed out in another big chair. All the others were sprawled in the other rooms behind closed doors. Sweeney said that the downstairs door was unlocked. Then there was dialogue that went pretty much as follows:

Me: Sweeney, damn man, what are you doing here, uninvited, but welcomed anyway?

Then I thought, this motherfucker is looking for Frenchy. Uh oh!
Sweeney: You know, Lincoln, this is completely unacceptable in every way.
Me: Excuse me, but I think what's unacceptable is you telling me what should happen in my home. But that's okay, acceptable or not to you, this is the shit that's happening. Please have a seat. You can squeeze in on the sofa next to Jenna's big ass.

Sweeney just stood and looked around the room. He looked disturbed as he studied the room. He walked over to a bookshelf, looked disapprovingly at a Campari poster that featured a nearly nude, nymphish lady invitingly holding a bottle.
Me: Sweeney, sitting next to that big pretty ass may do you some good; pulling that sheet up may do wonders. I think she ain't got no knickers on.

He was becoming irritated. I was laughing.
Sweeney: I will stand. I will not be here long. I am looking for Jean. He did not show up for breakfast this morning, and I know you have

become friends, and I fear he may have come under your wicked influence which gives cause to believe that he may have been here.
Me: Oh, Frenchy, he's still here. You don't recognize the back of his head?
Sweeney: What are you talking about?

Then I got up and stood above the sofa to my left where Frenchy and Suzette were sprawled. Earlier while cleaning, I had draped a sheet over them. One could see Suzette's head, but Frenchy's head was still face down on Suzette's bottom. I had been careful not to cover Frenchy's head as I did not want to disturb his enviable position, and I certainly did not want him to be lacking air. Sweeney had been straining not to see our surroundings by maintaining a stiff neck, and keeping his eyes mostly riveted on me as we spoke.
Me: Here he is.

As I pulled the sheet back revealing that Suzette's red panties were now further down her hips than they had been previously, and with my experienced eyes, I could see that at some point Frenchy had awakened, or perhaps in his sleep, indulged himself in Suzette's groceries. Upon seeing this, Sweeney let a loud combination gulp-whimper-shriek, somewhat highly pitched. It was the strangest sound that I had ever heard coming from a human being.
Me: Uh...you all right, Sweeney? I think you should sit.

Without noticing what he was doing, he slowly lowered himself on the sofa next to Jenna. The man was in shock, and I was trying hard not to laugh out loud. Then Sweeney became sad, almost crying. I really couldn't figure that shit out. Was he sad to see such sin? Did he feel like he had failed as a religious mentor of sorts? Was he wishing it was his tongue in that ass or any ass? Was he making a mental record of what he was seeing to retrieve once back in his Opus Dei masturbatorium?
Me: Sweeney! Sweeney! Snap out of it.
Sweeney: Jean!

Then louder, and louder.
Sweeney: Jean! Jean!

Frenchy begin to respond. When he looked up and saw Sweeney he was clearly embarrassed. Suzette started to awaken. I

hastily made sure she was covered.
Me: Desmond, I must ask you not to shout. People are sleeping.
Sweeney: I have to remove him from this den of yours now! This is a shameless spectacle beyond belief.
Me: Just wait a minute. You are out of line. This is my house, our house. You don't come up in here shouting, giving orders, denouncing, or saying who has to go. Jean is a man. All here are men and women. It is you who must leave. I'll ask you once more to speak quietly and respect my home.

Sweeney reached into his sport coat pocket and handed me an envelope.
Sweeney: This is your bill from your stay.
Me: Thank you Desmond. And we appreciate your hospitality.
Sweeney: I'm leaving. Jean. I will see you.
Me: He'll see you when he sees you.

Then Sweeney exited. By the time he had done so, several guests were awakening. Julio emerged from behind a closed door saying that he heard everything, as he yawned and laughed at the same time. In a few minutes everyone was up, and coffee, toast, ham, jam, and champagne were served. Suzette and Frenchy unraveled from one another and Suzette joined the queue for the toilette. Sweeney's performance was the topic of morning conversation and partially the cause of a merry morning filled with laughter. Frenchy said he would probably be asked to leave Sweeney's and asked if he could stay with us if that happened. I told him that he didn't have to be asked to leave: perhaps he should go to Sweeney's, pack his bag, go into Sweeney's office, and announce his immediate departure. Which is exactly what he did. Sweeney had failed at corralling this young man's spirit, further indoctrinating him into absurd, hypocritical, Catholic bullshit. We were not on a mission, but I'm happy that were pivotal in showing Frenchy a liberating good time that hurt no one. He later confessed that he was a virgin, but for years had fantasized about using a beautiful woman's ass as a pillow. Tossing her salad seemed natural once in the vicinity, he said. I agree.

What a night, Beau. Y'all opened your doors to the world, and the world came, and some stayed awhile. What happened next on your Amsterdam adventure?

Over the next few days, people from the dinner stopped by including Hans, the man who hadn't been out since World War Two, and Annemieke, the journalist. We left the downstairs door open so that we would not have to get up and ring the buzzer to let them in. People just came and knocked. Door was always open. We had no telephone, so impromptu visits were the order of the day.

I mentioned earlier that there was a bit of unrest going on in Amsterdam that summer. Julio and I got caught in the middle of a riot once, and I was forced to snatch a mounted policeman from his horse to prevent him from hitting us in with his club. I was concerned about repercussions from the cops but nothing happened. However, one night, I think I may have run into him. Ellie, Greece, a guitarist who we met at the dinner, and I decided to play music in the street as we were totally broke. I had the idea that outside the Concertgebouw would be an ideal location, entertaining concert-goers with a little blues as they exited. We were jamming, getting paid, and having fun. Ellie danced around to the music holding a hat out for contributions. Suddenly, two policemen appeared, flatfoots. They demanded passports, said what we were doing was illegal, called the wagon, and took us to jail. I mean no one I know– no musician, street performer, or beggar at that time ever heard of someone getting arrested for busking.

That kind of treatment seems out of character from the Amsterdam police, especially in that period. Do you think there was some other motivation for your treatment, other than what you were accused of?

I do. The more I thought about it, I was convinced that one of those cops was the one I yanked from his horse during a demonstration. They were far too aggressive. Normally, almost anywhere, a cop would tell you that street performance is not allowed, so move along. Also, they could have been just two racist cops who didn't like what they saw, Blacks and Whites together enjoying themselves. The Dutch invented apartheid in South Africa and enforced it with unimaginable cruelty. The connection between white South Africans and the Dutch is strong, involving generations of families, and businesses. The pillaging of natural resources, gold, diamonds, and crimes against humanity like slavery, murder, and rape were essential to satisfy the immense greed of the Dutch and the British in southern Africa. It's interesting to experience the quaint but modern, orderly Dutch society built on the blood, sweat, and natural wealth and resources of the people of their former colonies. So, us being thrown in jail may have been motivated by several factors, probably the least significant being what we were doing—playing music.

What happened after of your arrest?

We were all released from jail the following morning and given Exit Slips to give to immigration officials when we left the country. This had to take place within 30 days. Again, this was highly irregular. Not knowing what legal options may have been available, and thinking ahead to Paris anyway, all of us decided to leave Amsterdam and head to Paris within the 30-day period. Julio, Ellie, Greece, and I headed to Paris. Our other friends who had been visiting headed in different directions. The Amsterdam living experience of 1969 was over.

Chez J. F. Fabiano
Sainte-Sauveur-des-Monts, Québec
14-17 August, 2014

How were your first days in Paris?
The first day and night were tough. We had very little money– one hundred dollars between us. Parisians were still on their August holidays, and much of the city was closed. After one meal shared by the four of us, our money was cut in half. That was not enough money for a hotel, hostel, or anything else. We decided to walk from Gare du Nord to the Quartier Latin, as that may be our only hope to find a place to stay.
What kind of place with no money?
We had heard from people in Montreal that there was a Diggers house in Paris near Rue Mouffetard. Diggers came into existence in San Francisco in the mid-sixties as an alternative to youth hostels and cheap hotels. Some of their branches gave away food, organized concerts, provided childcare, tutoring, free healthcare. They were considered anarchist, communist, freethinkers, witches, and other paranoia-fueled nonsense propagated by some far-right conservative politicians and religious hypocrites. Usually, you paid what you could afford. Some Digger's accommodations were quite nice with private rooms and baths; others were more communal. Some were subsidized by grants or donations. There was a network around the U.S., Canada, and Europe.
It's an exhausting walk from the Gare du Nord to the Left Bank.
Oh, yeah, and we were already tired when we left Amsterdam. We had a little farewell soiree that left us with hangovers and little sleep. And we didn't sleep on the train. By the time we hit Boulevard Sainte-Michel, we were broke, hungry, raggedy, and dirty. No showers.
Broke and hungry, raggedy and dirty. That sounds familiar.
Yeah, now that I think about it. John Lee "Sonny Boy Williamson" wrote a song that goes:
I'm broke and I'm hungry, raggedy and dirty too,
If I clean up pretty mama, can I spend a little time with you?
That's what was happening. And it didn't get any better as evening

turned into night and we discovered after our long, hot, August walk that the Diggers were no more. Gone.
What next?
    We decided that not much more could be done other than to stay up all night or find a hideaway to flop in, but where was the question. We headed to Place Sainte-Michel and sat near the fountain. Imagine how we looked. We were three black men, well over six feet tall, with a pretty blonde white girl around five feet tall. We had one suitcase between us that we men took turns lugging around. No wheels. The rest of our bags were checked with the consignes at Gare du Nord. I had a plan but it was too late to act upon it, and it was Sunday evening. But Monday, everything would change. We all agreed that this night would be memorable and would never happen again. We headed to Pont Sainte-Michel and descended underneath the bridge where there is a walkway along the quay, occasional steps, and platforms that are large enough for one to huddle down on and try to sleep. Yes, we four were homeless that evening. Ellie covered herself with a sweater of mine from our bag, then used the bag for a pillow. The rest of us just huddled in the dark dampness on a ledge and steps. We were not alone under the bridge; there were several regulars who welcomed us and shared red wine from plastic bottles.
You managed to get some sleep, maybe just enough to revitalize?
    Just enough. But all of us wretches beneath the bridge were awakened at sunrise by the police, who knew several of the others by name. The police just looked at our peculiar configuration of three black men and a white woman and to our surprise said nothing more than "*Reveillez-vous et allez partir d'ici!*"
    And move along we did. Disheveled, hungry, broke, and stinky, we went to a nearby cafe in Place Sainte-Andre des Arts and with the few francs we had left, drank coffee and shared a croissant between us. This was *Les Miserables* re-lived, only 1969.
What was your plan?
    Okay. Ellie and I would go to Gare du Nord and get fresh clothes from our bags. Ellie would make use of shower facilities, and I would do a hoe's bath in a sink. Once cleaned up, Ellie and I would pose as a married couple and check into a hotel classy enough so that

one didn't have to pay up front or make a deposit. After we checked in we would sneak in Julio and Greece so they could clean up and get some sleep. The hotel was The Excelsior on Boulevard Sainte-Michel. Thank goodness this was before credit cards had to be used to get a room. All you needed was a passport and a good look, and Ellie and I were a stunning couple. And back in those days passports were kept at least overnight so they could be checked by police. The true window without payment was about thirty-six hours, enough time to get something together.

Julio and Greece must have been delighted?

To say the least. Those cats wanted to sleep for hours as did Ellie and I, but I had to wake them up. We were all exhausted, but it was important to get in touch with Claude Delcloo and clinch that record deal. Also, we needed money, so Ellie and I implemented phase two of my plan. Ellie and I went to the American Express office on Rue Scribe near Place de l'Opera. Ellie disguised herself to be pregnant. Back at that time on the second floor near the escalator was where clients could change money, cash traveler's checks, and do other financial transactions. There were usually a few people standing in line for a teller. After completing their transaction, customers would exit down a short hallway to the right where there was a flight of stairs leading to the ground floor. In this hallway there was a sofa, which is from where Ellie and I operated.

Operated?

That's correct. As people walked past us, we randomly selected individuals that looked like candidates to listen to our story, which was that we were on our honeymoon and had everything stolen from our hotel room during a fire alarm, even receipts for traveler's checks. Most took pity, some didn't even stop to listen. Some were happy to speak English with someone. Some looked disapprovingly at a black-white couple. It was about numbers. Out of every twenty hits we scored around $100. In some cases, we exchanged information, like names and addresses back in the States. And that was good, because some folks got a shock when they received a holiday card with ten or twenty bucks six months later. All and all, this was an essential element of our turning point from being bridge trolls. In four hours, we had around 1500 Francs, and 200 in

U.S. currency. Broke, hungry, raggedy, and dirty no more.

That's good money, especially back then when Paris was less expensive. What was the next move?

The next move was hardly expected. Ellie and I were about to head back to the *rive gauche*. As we were about to get up from the sofa, a tall, strapping, extremely well-dressed, 50-something white man approached, who by his manner could only be taken as a distinguished gentleman. He said he had just noticed us sitting there and wanted to know if we were okay or waiting for money. Waiting for money was not unusual. In those days, like for decades before, receiving money sometimes took ages. The only ways to get money were through the post, Western Union, American Express, orthrough a bank. Nothingwas instant. Sometimes it took a week for a telex to be approved and for the funds to arrive then be released. All Western Union transfers went through a distribution point in Cincinnati, and there things could be delayed for days for whatever reason.

Before I could answer that I was waiting for money, the gentleman introduced himself. His name was J. C. Calhoun and was the Administrator of the Paris American Express office. He was the top man. I hoped that he had not witnessed Ellie and me working the clients. After a while it was apparent that he had not, and was more concerned that we had been given proper service. He was curious about us though, and when I said I was a blues musician, he invited us into his well-appointed, luxurious office.

Just like that. In a matter of a few moments you went from requesting help from American Express customers to sitting with the Administrator.

That's right, and just 12 hours earlier, we had been rousted from beneath Pont Sainte-Michel. Life! Something else!

In Calhoun's office were paintings, little statutes, and numerous awards and certificates on the wall. There was also a trumpet case on a table. I asked Calhoun if he played. He said he did, and he loved Dixieland and blues. We talked about blues, Chicago, and how I was just beginning my career. This was the beginning of what would become an enduring friendship. About a week later I introduced Julio to Calhoun, and over the next couple of years the three of us did lots of hanging out at the Cafe de la Paix in Place de l'Opera. We had some great lunches. One afternoon he brought Liza Minnelli to lunch with us. She's great. Good conversation, sense of humor. And she had to be that way to be hanging with Calhoun, a real "Mr. Good Times." And so many times at the Cafe de la Paix, drinks were on the house. Julio and I were regulars for about two years, and during that time we became good friends with Marty, an Englishman, who was the lead bartender, who was London-Paris street hep on many levels. Marty eventually opened or took over a pub near the Champs Elysees, the Red Lion. And of course, we became known by management and the entire staff, from *les Garçons* to telephone operators upstairs who would send a bellboy to summon you if you had a call, or bring a phone to your table. Either way, this was extremely impressive to those unfamiliar with this system, especially to American tourists. There were a few occasions when I was sitting at my usual table with my Afro going in every direction, sunglasses, and a three-piece suit.

You had the look maybe of a Black Panther in a suit?

That's right. On one occasion, I recall that I was being stared at constantly by a middle-aged white American couple, and it was obvious that they are wondering about me, and that I was making them uncomfortable. A black man in the five-star Cafe de la Paix was not what they expected to see. During my travels, I've actually met a few Americans and Brits who've told me that part of the reason they were vacationing was to get away from black people for a while.

Seriously?

Ah yes. Happened to me a short time ago in Portugal. That's exactly what an English hag said to me at a tennis Club in Vilamoura. I responded that it was giving me great pleasure to fuck up her vacation. And I added that it is most unfortunate that were not laws prohibiting someone with a mug as ugly as hers, and legs to match, from wearing a tennis skirt.

Anyway, the bellman brings me the phone. The Americans gawk. I can see perplexity in their faces. Speaking normally into the telephone, they could detect that I was speaking an English-French blend. When I finished my conversation, Mademoiselle Benoit, the cigarette and cigar lady, brought me my usual afternoon cigar, a

Davidoff Number 2, and within minutes, Marty sent over a glass of champagne. The Americans, unaccustomed to such courtesies and politeness in their own world, especially extended to a Black, seemed further confounded.

Knowing you, this was amusing, right?

I was cracking up inside. I mean these people were having lunch with Coca Cola, and *patate fritte*, French fries, because they were in France. I decided to heighten their Paris experience by sending them a glass of champagne. "We didn't order that! We're not paying for that!" "*Ca c'est avec les compliments de Monsieur Black...S'il vous plait.*" "Huh?" said the man. In English, the waiter reiterated: "With the compliments of Monsieur Black." They looked toward me; I raised my glass in a toast accompanied by a slight nod of the head. They finally smiled and returned the gesture, but without grace. Marcel pulled my table out so that I could depart. As I walked toward the door, the American man caught up with me and said predictably, "Are you American?" I replied, "A boo-hunk-anunu-yaba-bola-lola-boo-hapsu!" or some other made up syllables. "Huh." He went back to his table. I strolled onto Boulevard des Capucines thinking hopefully, they had derived some benefit from that little encounter. Maybe just for a moment they could rethink how they view black people– and how incredibly underexposed they were.

I'm sure you had many such experiences wherever you traveled outside of the United States.

For sure. And you know some of those people would not give you the time of day in the U.S., but they are so insecure in another country, they chum up to people that may even hate because of familiarity.

Okay. Let's get back to you and Ellie.

Right. We left American Express and met up with Julio and Greece at the Hotel Excelsior. We had money, and had made a great contact. Now it was time to get with Claude Delcloo.

What happened with Delcloo?

When Ellie and I got back to the hotel, Julio had arranged a meeting with Delcloo at Storyville Jazz Bar that evening. We decided to pay the hotel for a week and upgrade to a suite. We went to dinner before meeting with Delcloo, and because we had been so hungry, for so long, food nearly drained us of all energy. Just the energy to digest was exhausting. But we moved forward with our plans.

Walking into Storyville was the most exhilarating and previously unknown event of my life. The four of us walked in, and several individuals looked towards the door to see who was making an entrance. When someone came in, people wanted to see who it was. Maybe someone from the media, a friend, or some jazz celebrity. We walked in and were unknown. We had on suits, straw hats, and a white girl with us. We were blues cats. Most of the people in the bar were New York jazz cats. They were decked out in dashikis, knitted skull caps, and other African-inspired attire. Looking down the bar was amazing: Don Cherry, Alan Silva, Frank Wright, Noah Howard, Arthur Jones, Clifford Thornton, Dave Burrell, Big Marva Broome, Bobby Few, Val Mathis, Sonny and Linda Sharrock, Claude Delcloo, The Pressure, and holding court at the rear was Archie Shepp surrounded by fans and women. Archie was decked out in a pinstripe, dark, blue three-piece suit, topped off with an African Kufi hat and Old Man Comforts on his feet. And mingled among the people I've mentioned were all kinds of other people. Then there were people seated along the wall at little tables. There were maybe sixty people squeezed into a small space where thirty could have fit comfortably.

So y'all couldn't even sit down?

Well, here's how it went. We knew no one in the joint. And I think because we were not dressed Afro-centric, the cats were a little suspicious, like maybe we were cops. Negro undercover agents sent to spy on black people abroad; black revolutionaries who may be communists. There were a few Black Panthers in Paris, and most of the people in the bar had been at the Pan-African Festival in Algeria. Algeria at the time was a haven for the Black Panther Party. So yeah, Negroes in suits were suspect.

Claude Delcloo looked up and recognized us and immediately came toward us, embracing us all. Going down the line, Delcloo made introductions, introducing Julio and me as Chicago Bluesmen. I got to tell you, some of them motherfuckers had thought we were cops, now they thought we were gangsters. Chicago blues gangsters.

Why gangsters?

They instinctively didn't trust people in suits. Archie was an exception because he is a multi-stylist, blending ethnic elements with Eurocentric tradition, and musically, he was at the top of his game. I can appreciate where the cats were coming from, especially in a group situation. It's like they were mumbling, "Who these motherfuckers?" But they would find out that we were all about business. Serious motherfuckers when it came to doing business and learning how to deal in France. That was gradual, but several benefited from our approach. So the gangster perception is tied to Chicago folklore about gangsters, and you know how it is in the hood: names and images just catch on, stick in people's minds. And Paris was becoming a hood itself, taking on characteristics of its inhabitants. "Them two is probably gangsters!"

And with Delcloo?

Well, we couldn't talk business in Storyville. Too many people around—no privacy. The four of us walked around the corner to the Cafe le Petit Pont, where we could sit quietly and talk. Ellie and Greece took a walk while Julio and I discussed with Delcloo. Delcloo had already discussed us with Jean-Luc Young, one of the owners of BYG records. He said he wasn't sure about the money for a first record, but to come out to the BYG office in the morning, and certainly, we could make a deal and get an immediate advance.

There was no negotiating?

No, not yet. But it was good to get to know Delcloo a bit, and we hadn't had any contact with him since we passed through Paris in June. I mean, a lot of cats didn't like Delcloo. I think because he was actually doing something and wanted to get something out of what he was doing. He wanted to benefit, not only musically but also his ego; he wanted to make history. He created opportunity, and a lot of cats were pissed off that they had to go for the money, and often, as part of the deal, Decloo would play drums on the recording sessions, as was the case with alto saxophonist Arthur Jones. And he was also the producer of most of the BYG-Actuel series.

I just want to be sure that I'm understanding this all correctly. Delcoo was producer, and he was responsible for bringing artists to the label. But he was not the money man?

That's right. Also, Jacques Bisceglia, the photographer and Storyville bartender, was responsible for bringing artists to the label. They were both often the target of cats' anger if the money situation didn't go down right. And that did happen sometimes, but it never happened to me with BYG. Others, yes. Remind me to share a story with you later about cats not getting paid.

What happened at the BYG office?

This was an amazing experience. The office was located near the Arc de Triomphe; I think it was on Avenue Kleber or Victor Hugo. The streets in this section of Paris are lined with elegant office buildings and apartments, probably built decades before World War Two. BYG was in such a building: both interior and exterior were stunning. This was all completely new to Julio and me. We ascended an ornate staircase towards the unmistakable sound of laughter and musicians speaking English. A brass sign with black lettering on a double door read BYG, Entree S.V.P. The door opened unto a reception area with offices to the left, right, and behind. There were musicians everywhere, walking the halls, sitting on chairs and sofas, and seated at the desk with two receptionists, telling them how fine they are. Some were counting banknotes; some were talking about changes to their contracts. The place was lively and happy. Upon opening the door, a chime notified the receptionists and Delcloo of our arrival. Delcloo emerged and instantly several musicians that we had met the night before at Storyville greeted us or commented on our arrival. "It's the Chicago brothers!" Greetings were exchanged and Delcloo ushered us immediately to Jean-Luc Young's office, which was bare except for his desk, several chairs, and a stereo system. With a handshake, and without hearing a note, Jean-Luc proposed an exclusive three-record deal over three years. Of course, there was legalese in the contract in French, accompanied by what I would later discover to be an inaccurate translation in English. No matter. Everybody there was signing whatever, just to get their hands on some cash. Jean-Luc had several signed contracts on his desk from new signers like Sunny Murray, Alan Silva, Grachan Moncur lll, and others. He flashed them in such a way that we couldn't see amounts, only names, so that we would be impressed and sign. I agreed and signed with a $2,000 advance. Jean-Luc called another office and said in English to please pay Chicago Beau $2,000. A woman appeared at the door and had us follow her to another office. On her desk there were several piles of Francs in different denominations. She counted out 10,000 Francs in five hundred, hundred, and fifty Franc banknotes. In Francs, it looked like a lot of money to us. In reality it was enough to get by for a while. It was necessary to stay on the case and not let up.

Still, what was it, 48 hours before you were sleeping under Pont Sainte-Michel?

Yeah, I was deeply grateful. I'm still grateful, and will always be. But basically, in retrospect, as I was learning more about the business, strictly from that point of view, that was not a good deal. Not only not for me, but for some of the others as well. But I was 20 years old, and this is the very last thing that I was expecting to happen to me. Also, Jean-Luc was just a little older than me; maybe he was 22 or 23, so none of our thinking was on the ball. He was having a heck of an experience though, and he had the capital to do it, up to a point.

You've got a record deal, what's the next step?

Okay, I signed and got $2,000 in advance for Chicago Beau's Blues Band, and BYG was supposed to bring in musicians from Chicago or wherever for the recording session and pay them separately. $2,000 was not much money to pay a band, just me. Well, no more money came from Jean-Luc to bring in and pay musicians. After awhile, it was decided to go with a French band lead by saxophonist Marc Richard. We got together in the studio, and honestly, it was horrible. I mean we all could play, just not together. And J.C. Calhoun from American Express was on the session playing trumpet. He was there for the thrill of it. I told the producer, Pierre La Tesse, that I had to have a Chicago Band, some real blues cats. That never happened, and the jazz cats around Paris were not the ones to try and cover Muddy Waters or Sonny Boy.

What happened to the three-record deal?

Without a band, there was nothing that could be done. Julio and I later discovered some rock cats around and some veteran R&B players. The only real Bluesman on the scene at that time was Memphis Slim, and later, things would come together with him.

I think one reason a proper session never happened is that BYG was becoming over extended and money rumors abounded among the musicians. BYG had been giving out advances, and doing lots of recording, but according to what cats were saying, sometimes the next round of cash didn't happen. And it's well known that they were operating at a loss, especially after the festival in Amougies, Belgium. So, my record deal just dissolved from both ends.

What happened next?

During that period, Julio and I got to know Archie Shepp. He came by a club one night and heard us blowing acoustically with some local cats. He walked up said that he was doing a bluesy thing for BYG, and that he would like to use two harmonicas in opposing keys. The next evening, we met at the studio. It was a hell of a moment for me. Archie hadn't said who was going to be on the session. Dig this: Jeanne Lee, vocals; Lester Bowie, trumpet; Philly Joe Jones, drums; Dave Burrell, piano; Malachi Favors, bass, Archie Shepp, tenor sax; Julio Finn and me, harmonica.

Y'all in there with the top of the line!

I'm telling you. And that recording, *Blasé*, has survived the test of time. I've read all kinds of critiques about that music. Some love it, others hate it. Some think that the harps being in different tuning was a mistake by Julio and me. I mean, those who criticize the harp tuning are so dumb and full of themselves that they never stop to think that Archie Shepp wanted things that way, and you have to always remember– a good number of music critics and reviewers are just re-scribbling some other re-scribbler's scribbling. And so I consider this date to be the beginning of my professional music career: August 16, 1969.

All right. You got your record deal and some cash. How long did you stay in the Hotel Excelsior and what was the next move?

LaBosse, things were moving at dazzling speed. Ellie needed to go to California on some personal matters. And though she never said this, I believe she may have had enough of our wild and highly unpredictable way of living. She was always there though, a real trooper– a person with a wide and beautiful soul. After the first week was over in the hotel, we decided to split up. Ellie moved into a smaller hotel on Boulevard Sainte-Michel and got some needed privacy. I gave her some cash to shop and get a ticket home. Years would go by before we'd meet again. You know, very different journeys.

Ellie was always with y'all, but you haven't said if she was romantically involved with any of you.

No, she wasn't. Occasionally people would ask that. And you how people can be, what they can imagine. All kinds of sexual scenarios that are far from the truth were suggested by some. We dismissed them as idiots. Ellie was a dear friend, and that was that.

And after Ellie left?

Shortly after Ellie's departure, Maurice decided to return to the States, to Florence, Alabama, to spend time with his fragile and aging grandmother. I think that was a good move as he was not cut out for the uncertainties of a life of adventure, chance, and guidance by the Cosmics. In our days in Québec he was much more comfortable, but crossing the Atlantic and putting that great of a distance between himself and his family was, for the most part, more than he could handle. And his people were not pleased at all. Their lives were zip-code centered; the idea of visiting another continent was totally incomprehensible. His dilemma overwhelmed him, and it became increasingly obvious that he couldn't thrive for long outside of familiar surroundings. I think by mid-September they were both gone.

With them gone, what were the next moves for you and Julio?

As I said, things were moving fast. We moved from the Excelsior to the Hotel Sainte-Jacques, and over the next couple of months to several other hotels. Occasionally, one of us would find another situation, like the accommodations of a lady friend.

Now, you're getting established on the scene, as well as the others. Who stands in your mind as a major player or influence on the scene?

Good question that must be treated at some length. Here, regrettably, I have to departmentalize a bit. Different people had different agendas. The New York cats, seemingly lead by Frank Wright and his boys Bobby Few, Noah Howard, and Muhammad Ali, had a strong following. For a while they were migratory, moving from cafe to cafe with their band of followers. At first it was Storyville, then the Chat Qui Pêche, pronounced Jackie Page by some cats, where fights broke out sometimes. Then the Cafe Mabillon for a few months, and finally they found a permanent roost at Le Select on Boulevard Montparnasse, across from La Couple. On almost any evening when they weren't performing or out of town, they could be found there along with other New York cats like Alan Silva, Bob Reid, Arthur Jones, Nigerian Pablo Savage, Alan Shorter, and an assortment of women and hangers-on. Of that Frank Wright group, pianist Bobby Few adjusted well to Parisian life, and has been living in France since 1969. In fact, he has become a beacon on the French jazz scene and is a highly regarded as a teacher and spiritual conduit through music.

Archie Shepp had another scene happening. He had a large apartment on Rue de l'Université. There, others would hang out when he allowed it. I was there on several occasions. I remember once when BYG had failed to pay musicians for gigs or recordings, a strategy session was held at Shepp's. Present among several were Cal Massey, Hart Leroy Bibbs, Earl Freeman, Clifford Thornton, Julio Finn, Alan Silva, Yasmina and Joseph Jarman from the Art Ensemble of Chicago. At this session, Hart Leroy Bibbs was the most rational and vocal about how to get paid. But others there preferred almost military type action. Earl Freeman, seated at an architect's table and wearing a Snoopy pilot's cap and a green military jumpsuit, drew up plans for a raid in the BYG offices.

Did they actually raid the offices?

Hell, yeah! Led by Earl Freeman. One morning as soon as the office opened, a group of about ten New York cats bursts into the office threatening secretaries, Jean Luc, and everybody else. They stood on desks, kicked over chairs, grabbed a few people. Earl Freeman, who always walked around with a long bullwhip, cracked that whip at everything and everybody. Then Georgakarakos came out and shouted, "Stop, I'll pay!" And he did. My understanding is that BYG kept large amounts of cash around the office. They had already learned not to even think about paying people with a check, which wasanold trick used by some French people in the music business. They would give you a crossed check: that's two lines drawn across the upper left-hand corner of a check. That meant they could only be deposited in one's bank account. Now, those motherfuckers knew full well that musicians having recently arrived didn't have bank accounts, or even the necessary credentials to get one. Of course, you would have to chase them down, sometimes for months to get your money, if at all. The only other solution was having a French person deposit the check in their account, and certainly, in such a short period of time, those types of relationships had not been developed by most of the cats. BYG knew that the sight of a checkbook might spell disaster for them all. They had cash! Still, it took the threat of violence to get paid. It's good he paid them because Frank, Muhammad, and those cats were rough. I mean one reason for their migration was sometimes they would get into fights and turn a cafe out. Of course, had they hurt BYG people they would have ended up in jail. I'm glad it all worked out.

What other scenes were going on?

There were the Chicago cats. They had a whole different approach to being in Paris. The Art Ensemble of Chicago had come over on the last voyage of the USS United States with two vans and all of their equipment. Lester Bowie had his family, Fontella Bass, and kids. I think Bahnamous was born in Paris. They had a no-nonsense approach to the business. They proceeded to quickly establish a recognizable Art Ensemble Brand. They were inclusive of French artists and quickly developed a relationship with singer-songwriters Brigitte Fontaine and Areski, who were well known in France. They collaborated on music, film, and theater projects. They were successful as a group and individually. They rented a huge country house in Sainte-Leu-la Forêt where they could rehearse, maintain a garden, and live in comfort. I remember the first time I went there: Fontella put my hair in braids and Lester was working the kitchen. Out back somebody was practicing a sax. That was the AEC home. Just down with it and homey.

Another cat from Chicago was Anthony Braxton. He maintained a low profile, but was highly effective as an innovator or composer. He gravitated toward academic circles and is a chess master. Not long ago he received a Genius Grant from the MacArthur Foundation. In Braxton's circle were Leroy Jenkins and Steve McCall, extremely pleasant cats and a pleasure to be around.

The Chicago cats didn't have a money problem with BYG?

No, they didn't as far as I know. But they had other problems, and as they came up, they chose more conventional methods to resolve them. As I said, they were deeply involved with established French artists, and one of the advantages of that was access to resources when needed. So if something had gone wrong with BYG, they would have figured out a way to resolve it without an assault on their offices.

Who is next in your departmentalizing?

There were the "Independents" who got along with most. However, there were some complete mad men among them. Talented and troubled Alan Shorter walked around with a golf club and occasionally attacked people on the street or in a cafe. He was out of it. He needed treatment. Also, I don't believe he would have been doing that crazy shit in the U.S.; cops or somebody would have shot him. And Earl Freeman unleashed his bullwhip at the masses more than once. His behavior became so bizarre that unfortunately he spent some time in jail in Rouen. Like Alan, he was troubled.

There was the congenial Steve Potts who easily assimilated into Parisian life and remains a bright light in the Paris music scene. Ken Tyler, a wonderful drummer, maintained a low profile and was effective doing his thing. Other Independents were Ken Terroade, Dave Burrell, Steve Lacy and his wife, Irene Aebi, Sunny Murray, Jerome Cooper, Big Marva Broome, and Ray Draper.

Famoudou Don Moye from Rochester, New York, was a staunch Independent. Then he became the drummer-percussionist with the Art Ensemble. He moved from an Independent to becoming a major force in one of the greatest jazz groups of all time. And as a solo artist, he's considered one of the greatest percussionist of all time, having received numerous awards internationally.

Now Julio and I were Independents who moved through many sectors of the Paris scene, from all the black music clusters, to the Alain Delon crowd, to the Chez Castel and Regine's crowd, the Gilbert Becaud circle, and the established Black Master Elders that included artists, scholars, attorneys, restaurateurs, and other professionals.

Who were the Black Elders?

All right. These were black people in the arts, and other businesses that had become successful and an integral part of the international community in France. They were officially and unofficially ambassadors of black culture. Josephine Baker, Tria French, Memphis Slim, Johnny Griffin, Kenny Clark, Art Taylor, L. Compton Kolawole, Rhoda Scott, Mickey Baker, Turner O'Neal, Willie Mabon, Hart Leroy Bibbs, Art Simmons, Freddie Red, Leroy Haynes, Beauford Delaney—and not always on-the-scene people like Clifford Jordan and James Baldwin. There were others, but these come to mind right now.

What do you mean by successful?

They were masters of their craft who had in most cases become a part of the French or other European system. Some purchased homes, married or partnered with French or other European or African Nationals, owned businesses such as nightclubs and restaurants. They had become a respected part of the economic community in France, generating jobs and revenue. An example is Leroy Haynes, who owned a soul food restaurant in Paris since the fifties. Every major act that came to town at some point over the years had dinner at Haynes.' Willie Mabon was a partner in the Chevalier du Temple club and restaurant. Tria French was a talent agent; she got me an acting job in one of the National Theater Companies with Antoine Bourseiller in Marseille, then Paris. Turner O'Neal was a successful International Law attorney. Memphis Slim was a silent partner in several ventures. He had a regular gig at Aux Trois Mailletz near Rue Petit Pont in the *Quartier Latin*, but when he played concerts in huge venues near Paris, like in Versailles, it would be sold out. He was the most successful resident musician in Paris.

James Baldwin had an incredible following. When in Paris he usually stayed at the Hotel Sainte-Germain. He used to move up and down Boulevard Sainte-Germain stopping at the Cafe Mabillon, then continue along to the Cafe Flore. Usually, he was accompanied by an assistant, who for a while was a Chicago cat, Ray Frost. Ray and I became friends in Los Angeles years later, where on a near daily basis we paid tribute to the Belle Epoch lifestyle we had enjoyed in Paris.

These people rarely would be seen where you would see the BYG crowd. Of course, occasionally almost anyone could be playing at the Chat Qui Peche, or in concert, and that's when cats would show up and pay their respect to one another. Some afternoons Memphis Slim would sit the Cafe Petit Pont, around the corner from Aux Trois Mailletz, his Rolls Royce parked at the curb. It never took long for fans and musicians to recognize him and often join him on the terrace. Slim was always approachable when he was out and about. And Memphis Slim, you know, was made a Commander in the French *Ordre de Arts et des Lettres* by the Ministry of Culture. And the U.S. Senate honored him with the title of Ambassador-at-Large-of Good Will. His well-deserved recognition irritated some white people in blues business and press so much that in one of his obituaries it was written that because of living in France, his music had lost it roots feeling—comments from non-Black, arrogant, jealous, and odious scribblers.

Let me go back. We've got the New Yorkers and their followers led by Frank Wright. Then there were the Chicago cats, the Independents, and the Black Masters.

Well, as an extension of the Independents there were other artists who showed up occasionally for gigs. They were, for most part, too involved in what they were doing, and who they were doing it with, to hang out for long. When cats came through town for gigs, you might see them briefly at the Chat Qui Pêche or Storyville. Other in-town cats like Peter and Tony Clarke, who were performers in the Paris production of *Hair*, were rarely on the music scene. In later years, Peter changed his name to Clarke Peters and is having brilliant career as a singer, actor, dancer, author, playwright, film and theater director. He crafted an exquisite show called *Five Guys Named Moe* centered around the music of Louis Jordan. You see, cats like the Clarke brothers were part of the scene, but off into their own thing deeply. Not much time for hanging out. And in recent years, Clarke Peters starred in the HBO series, *The Wire*. Clarke's dealing!

Here I should mention an exceptionally creative human being: the painter Beauford Delaney. Beauford had been a fixture in Paris since the fifties, and he was a great friend of writer Henry Miller. They had known each other in New York years earlier. Much has been written about Beauford. To our readers I'm suggesting that they find a chapbook titled *The Amazing and Invariable Beauford Delaney* by Henry Miller. It's a loving and respectful tribute to a great artist by a great writer.

Who were your key influences on the scene?

Let me start with Memphis Slim. Slim's advice was simple: "Watch all these motherfuckers." Enacting it was a learning process. Slim said to always be cautious when dealing with blues promoters in Europe because they are used to dealing with uneducated cats as though they were children. He said to be sure to get paid up front and don't let them bully you. Stand your ground, and walk away from a gig if you mustto preserve your dignity. He was right. Through the years I've seen blues tours organized by a cluster of local promoters that featured several lead artists and a backup band, maybe ten people total. The gigs were well funded by local sponsors and sometimes government grants. However, what the musicians were paid was nothing short of twentieth-century slavery. Here's an example: a concert called something like American Blues Tour would pay around $40,000 dollars. That was the average. The tour would have ten concerts, that's $400,000. If 10 musicians got paid $1,000 each per concert, the entire salary budget would be $100,000 or 25 percent of budget. $300,000 remaining. Now the road managers, drivers made minimum $1,000 a week, and those guys were usually friends and family of the promoter. Ten concerts over two weeks is quite the norm. Okay, around $6,000 for them. Now we're at $294,000. Usually, the local organization had hotels as sponsors so the promoter didn't have to pay lodging. In cases when they did, they put blues people up in the funkiest one or two-star, shit-hole they could find: no private rooms, everybody doubled, even tripled up. Maybe if there was one lady on the tour, she would get a room.

Meals. Unless provided by the local organization, the musicians had to pay their meals, unless it was breakfast in the hotel, which is typically provided with a room. And here let me point out that musicians would have to load up bags, napkins, Tupperware containers, anything to put some food in, because they needed to eat and often couldn't afford the price of meals in a restaurant. Of course, the promoter would pay it for them and deduct it from their salary.

Transportation. By no means adequate. Usually a cargo van with hard-ass seats, bumping along kilometer after kilometer. The costs for two of these usually ugly white vehicles—around round

$2,000 for the entire tour. If they had been willing to spend another $1,000, they could have provided comfortable transportation. But keep in mind, to some of European promoters, like their American counterparts, blues people were nothing more than cargo. Let's take off $4000 for the vans total because there were often breakdowns. This brings the available budget down to $290,000. Now I said *if* the musicians got $1,000 per concert, right?

Right.

That never happened. They are usually paid by the week, not by concert. A blues lady from Detroit who I ran into on one of these blues shows in Limoges told me she was making $500 a week. She thought she was well paid, going home maybe after her own expenses with $700. So, let's break it down a bit. Ten people making a total of $10,000 for two weeks. A grand each. The real profit for the agent-promoter around is around $380,000. Slavery. Nothing but total exploitation.

Memphis Slim was schooling you on avoiding the pitfalls of doing business in France and elsewhere in Europe. It's well known in music business circles and among musicians that he hired or worked with over the years that he was rather crafty himself. He was very familiar with the ways of rascals, wouldn't you say?

Exactly. But the bad guys were the minority. And really, it was unhealthy to mess around with the New York cats' money. Then you had some folks who would try to be slick until you called them on it. Some of them did delayed wrong, like not paying royalties or misusing artists names. I had that happen with my album *Black Gypsy*. The album was supposed to be a poetry/jazz project. The agreed album title was *Black Gypsy*, Chicago Beau, featuring Archie Shepp, which was recorded on November 9, 1969. The initial release came out catalogued under Shepp's name. When you look at who wrote the music and lyrics, it's Augustus Arnold and Chicago Beau, the same with the liner notes. Pierre Berjot, who was also known as Pierre Jaubert, who I was introduced to and cautioned about by Memphis Slim, was the producer for America Records, also known as Musidisc Europe. I signed the contract, with Shepp agreeing to be a featured guest artist. When the record came out, Pierre lied and said it was a mistake made by record company executives at the top. Wasn't nobody believing that bullshit. But what could we do? Slim had warned me about him, but without specifics. So Pierre apologized and wanted to do more recordings. He wanted to record the Art Ensemble of Chicago, and an album with Philly Joe Jones as part of a series of poetry/jazz projects. The main thing about Pierre is that he did keep his word on the cash and showed up at the recording sessions with my money, so paying cats was never a problem. And he paid what was agreed. With him it was how the recordings were released. I composed tunes and lyrics, "Certain Blacks," and "One for Jarman," that were released as an Art Ensemble of Chicago album. The agreed album title was *Chicago Beau, Blues Poet, Meets the Art Ensemble of Chicago*. The album was released as an AEC album, after Pierre had promised this would not happen again. But again, the same lie, a decision at the top. I finally realized with my young twenty-year-old, naïve ass, that Pierre was a flim-flam, lying motherfucker who knew I would get the best musicians on my sessions. In the case of the AEC, *Certain Blacks* release, Pierre and Musidisc really fucked up the album info with misspellings, wrong names, and credits.

Did anything get resolved?

Pierre later told me that I and the other artists should be grateful to him because our music was recorded and it may not have been if it weren't for him– and that it didn't matter how the records were released because they would survive over time, and all would benefit, thanks to him. He was right about the music's survival, but using that line of thinking to justify his dishonesty reveals a diseased mind bordering on being criminal. A good thing is that I retain publishing and neighboring rights on all my recorded work. When Verve re-released *Black Gypsy*, *Certain Blacks*, and some other material, they paid. That's doing the right thing. However, *Black Gypsy* was released as a Shepp Album. Not right. As I said before, Shepp didn't need me to write his material. So, the rip-off continues. Over the course of nearly fifty years, since 1970, Verve has been the only record company that has paid on a re-release. Prestige Records refused to communicate when they re-released *Black Gypsy*. They wouldn't return phone calls, answer a letter, nothing. Cowards.

That's a shameful story which unfortunately has been retold too

many times by mainly black artists– treachery taking place at the hands of record companies, producers, and others in the music business.

Exactly. And Pierre did business with popular white rock artists. I can't say for certain, but I doubt that King Harvest or Creedence Clearwater were treated the same.

You had some dealings with King Harvest?

Ah, yes. The King Harvest guys were living outside Paris. Musically, they were essentially rock cats who had interest in blues. Ron Altbach, who in my mind was their leader, is an excellent classical music pianist and composer. They were all friends who had attended Cornell University together. They had a look that represented aspects of rebel White culture at that time, like The Band and Bob Dylan. Their album covers had them perched on motorcycles looking ready for adventure. But their look was a look that had nothing to do with the realities of their economic status and privileged social status as American white boys who had attended an Ivy League university with the intent of becoming professionals like doctors and lawyers. The appeal of music and the lifestyle they cultivated overwhelmingly redirected their priorities. I don't know about Didier, the French bass player's, background, but the Americans were from extremely affluent families. I'm not speaking about this as a fault; they just had never been in the trenches of survival. When you work with cats like that, you have to be mindful that y'all are coming from a different place, headed in very different directions. The hippy-look thing was just that, *a thing.* When it came to dealing with cash, their culture of money was utmost. But in my opinion they were spoiled and never felt the need to survive as do people coming from lesser circumstances. They struggled a bit like anybody trying to play music, but they had opportunities many people could only dream about. I mean, these cats had a mansionette outside of Paris that was outfitted with everything you need to take a rock band on the road. They had a hit that topped the charts called "Dancing in the Moonlight," and they had each other. One asks, what do you need to be successful and happy? I don't think there is a clear answer. But one great thing is that except for those who passed away, Wells Kelly and Doc Robinson, the King Harvest friendship remains strong after fifty years. I'm still in touch with Ron Altbach since 1969. He is a gentleman in every sense of the word, an astute businessman, and brilliant performer.

How was your musical relationship with King Harvest?

It was mostly fun and productive. We had some great gigs. They backed me as my Blues Band. I was being booked as the Chicago Beau Blues Band. The American Center concerts, the Nancy Jazz Festival and tour, and the Blue Note in Paris are among many fun gigs. Many of them played on Julio Finn's Barclay Records albums, *Rainbows All Over My Blues*, a silly title conceived in the brain of producer Philippe Rault, and *Deal For Service*. I did some vocals on both of those albums.

Pierre Jaubert was working with King Harvest you said?

That's right. He co-produced along with American music publisher Jack Robinson, *Dancing in the Moonlight*. Honestly, I don't know anything about the numbers in terms of how the money went down, but I'm reasonably certain that Pierre was watching his step when it came to dealing with King Harvest and subsequent dealings with their album. Nothing went down like what happened with the Archie Shepp and Art Ensemble recordings.

Interesting. Let's move on. How about gigs around Paris, around Europe?

Across Europe there were lots of opportunities. Jazz festivals and clubs abounded. There was always something going on in Paris. The Frank Wright Quartet, Art Ensemble of Chicago as a group and individually, Steve Lacy, Clifford Thornton, Archie Shepp, Dave Burrell, Marva Broome, Alan Silva, Willie Mabon, Memphis Slim. And then the South African cats Chris McGregor, Dudu Pukwana, and Mongasi. The brilliant percussionist and drummer, Jean-Francois Fabiano collaborated with everybody. He wasn't twenty yet, but his genius was recognized by the veteran players. And dancers, man! Sister Elsa from Senegal had a top-notch dance troupe that operated out of the American Center. The town was jumping. There was something happening at universities, night clubs, big and small theaters, private parties, the Museum of Contemporary Art, and other such institutions. Nearly every day, every night, there was something going on. Everyone was gigging.

There were interesting collaborations with all types of artists: painters, dancers, circus acts. Collaborations across cultures and languages. New Year's Eve 1972, I co-starred in a show at the Ranelagh Theatre in Paris called *Blues Dream*, written by poet Hart LeRoy Bibbs. It was a play, musical, and modern dance performance that included blues, jazz, visual art, and soul food collaboration. I've a flier here in the photo pages. Nothing but fun bringing in the New Year. Reverend Frank Wright, Julio Finn, Bob Reid, and a group called Emergency provided the music. At some point back in those days, I don't remember exactly when, Frank Wright added "Reverend" to his name. It was shortly after adding "Reverend" that his performances became more and more animated. He would jump on the floor and play on his knees, then jump and stand on a chair. From there he would sometimes jump on tables in the audience, knocking over drinks as he threw himself down or rolled around kicking, all the time blowing that tenor sax. I mean totally wild. He would usually do this to a tune he called "Church Number Nine" that was usually the closing number of the gig. And there were always blues licks woven into his sound. . . I mean his Mississippi Blues roots would emerge no matter how much he improvised. You know Frank also played electric bass and had worked with B.B. King and Bobby Bland. Yeah man, Frank Wright was a force to be dealt with in many ways.

Yeah, I remember seeing Frank Wright before he was the Reverend, and that was always exciting. Anyone else come to mind, other great performances or collaborations?

You know, the Art Ensemble of Chicago did some interesting collaborations. There was a very popular French duo, Brigitte Fontaine and Areski. The AEC worked with them in several situations including the soundtrack for a film, *Les Stances à Sophie*, that some people call their greatest collaboration—and greatest album. It is indeed a special recording that also included vocals and piano by Fontella Bass. I think it was recorded in 1970, which was at the height of the Paris Black Music Epoch, which in my thinking began at the close of The Great War. Right here, I want to suggest to our readers to check out *Great Black Music-Ancient to the Future*. It's a book I wrote in 1997 about the AEC and is available online. In the book, they speak in-depth about their France experience and a lot more.

Let's refresh the question I asked you a little while ago: who were your key influences? You started with Memphis Slim– who else?

Thanks for jolting my memory. Hart Leroy Bibbs introduced me to the literary scene. He knew publishers, editors, printers, booksellers, etcetera. He was well known in literary circles from James Baldwin to Jean Paul Sartre. He often read at Shakespeare and Company Books and produced literary events around Paris. We became friends the moment we met. He used to call me "the bedrock of these crazy-ass motherfuckers in Paris." And he called me that because despite my youthful learning errors, I did manage to get things done and get musicians paid. Spending time with Bibbs, I learned a lot about the nature of some of the cats I was dealing with as well as their experiences, which were completely new to me. Bibbs was from jazz haven Kansas City, Missouri, and had been living in New York for a few years. He knew the cats, and the French, and coached me as to how to deal with certain situations. I was inspired by his writing and photography. I vowed to one day publish his work, which I finally accomplished in 1988, nineteen years after we met, when I founded the literary magazine *Literati Chicago*. I want to add here that Leroy Bibbs and Dexter Gordon appeared in the film *Round Midnight*, made in 1986.

Exactly. Okay. Things seemed to be rolling well for you. Before we move on is there anything else you'd like to recall in this early Paris period?

Absolutely. As I said, things were moving at a rapid pace. A truly wonderful thing that happened during that period was falling in love and having a partner with whom to share the creativity and madness of the scene. One unusually sunny afternoon in September, Julio and I were strolling along Boulevard Sainte-Michel from the Jardin de Luxembourg heading toward Boulevard Sainte-Germain. Walking in the opposite direction on the other side of the street, we saw two beautiful young black women and paused to have a better look. They immediately noticed us and shouted out, "Hey brothers, hey brothers," and waved. We shouted back, "Sisters!" We beckoned them to come to us, and they beckoned us to come to them. We went to them. The ladies were Linda Carter and Betty Anne. Almost instantaneously, Linda and me had a thing for each other. Julio and Betty Anne didn't hit it off the same way. In fact, they weren't attracted to each other. But Linda and me... bam! It wasn't no intimate thing right away, but the vibe was there.

Y'all starting hanging tough?

Yeah, we did. Linda was reserved in the beginning. She and Betty Anne had come from Toronto to France to study. This trip they were on was a kind of reconnaissance mission to check out schools, job possibilities, and such. Linda's beauty was breathtaking. In my opinion, perfect in every way: statuesque, regal style, great dancer, articulate. A fine, fine woman. After we started hanging out and I learned more and more about her talents, I tried to convince her that she had too much going for herself to be in school. Her plans started to gradually unravel. Eventually, as we spent more and more time together, it became clear that school was not happening; she started considering auditioning for theatre, film, and dance gigs. Betty Anne eventually returned to Toronto.

How long before you and Linda decided that being together was the way it was going to be?

It was gradual, and I was determined. But you know—I was also playing it cool. I needed her to understand that I was thinking beyond the sexual possibilities and superficial posturing. The old school players I was around as a teen back in Chicago always said that when you find somebody you love, try to imagine life after the fucking is over, because that's who you gonna be with. As Linda and I got to know each other, I think for a moment she may have thought that I wasn't interested in her, but that wasn't hardly the case. I never let on, but my nose was open like a mug. But another thing was that she often spoke about her boyfriend, Eddie, back in Toronto, who was Betty Anne's brother. I nicknamed him The Novelist because he wrote Linda love letters of twenty-plus handwritten pages stuffed into two or three envelopes. Linda would receive a "serial" letter sometimes over two or three days. When she started reading his frantic proclamations aloud, I knew his place in her heart was rapidly vanishing.

He was working on your behalf and didn't know it. And some cats do that: they be driving their lady away by being too im-

posing. So, you were aloof and it paid off.

Oh, yes. Linda and I were always together and were perceived as an item by people on the scene. But I still hadn't made my defining swoop, and neither had she.

Come October, there was the BYG Music Festival in Amougies, Belgium. Julio and I were invited by the Art Ensemble to do a tune with them at the festival. About thirty of us rode up to Amougies on a tour bus provided by BYG. This was the most incredible bus ride I've ever experienced. On board were, and I can't remember everyone, Joseph Jarman, Earl Freeman, Claude Delcloo, Alan Silva, Kenneth Terroade, Louis Moholo, Malachi Favors, Jacques Bisceglia, friends, members of the press, boyfriends, girlfriends, and others that no one knew, like two young German women who were walking down the street and asked where the bus was going while loading in Paris. One of the cats told them about the festival. They waited to see if there was room, then they got on with what they had with them in backpacks. They were literally German tourists who stumbled upon a busload of musicians and decided to come along. They were ready for anything. It didn't take long for them to settle in with some of the cats. You know, they were choosing—cats were trying to get chosen.

Was that unusual behavior?

In Europe, outside of the U.S. and the jazz world, not really. Young women, white women, comfortably getting on a bus loaded with mostly black musicians, looking for adventure would be considered acceptable. You know in the States, all kinds of laws existed to protect white women from black men. But as typical Christian ethics dictate, there are no laws protecting black women from anything.

I hear you. So, adventure was sought and achieved?

That's right. They found some. They had a blast. What happened is the trip started out quiet, almost meditative. After about two hours on the road, Joseph Jarman took out a flute and began playing very softly, melodically. It wasn't long before he was joined by others playing various instruments. Wine and reefer appeared. The mood shifted from meditative to bus theatre. Cats stood in the bus aisle playing and swaying to the rhythm of the road. Somebody improvised a poem. Djembes came out and provided African backbeat to horn solos, hollers, recitations, and polyrhythms being created along the French autoroute. The German girls were in a state of bliss. By the time we reached the Belgian frontier, the bus had become a rolling asylum of free creative spirits inspired and intoxicated by music and life itself.

I'm sure crossing into Belgium was interesting. What happened? I know some shit happened.

As the bus approached the border, the tour manager, an employee of BYG, suggested that everybody calm down, pass their passports up to him, and he would try to get us into Belgium with as little hassle as possible. Everybody complied with the passport request, but most were too far gone, too high or just plain happy or crazy, to calm down. The fact that the bus came to a stop at the border crossing seemed to encourage more performance. Anyway, the BYG man got off the bus to deal with the Belgian officials. He explained what was going on, who we were, and so on. You've got to understand some of them Belgian officials' brains are locked in colonial thinking, you know– King Leopold shit. A bus load of black artists to them is a busload of *negres*. That means no respect and be prepared for bad treatment.

The Belgian royalty and military historically had been greedy, blood-thirsty, genocidal maniacs. Back in 1969, and now, they are still hanging to their ill-gotten gains in Africa. I can't imagine any kind of respect coming from border officials.

What happened was funny—to me any way. Two border officials boarded the bus, each with a handful of passports. Their intention was to go down the line calling out a name, then compare the person's face with the one on the passport. You know the old perpetrated racist white lie that we all look alike? Man, this was too much. They would call out, let's say, "Willie Perkins!" Willie would shout out, "Yeah." Then they would walk back, hold the passport near his face, then hold it near the face of others, to be sure they had the right negro, since we all look so similar. After two or three of these face comparisons, the musicians just erupted. "Fuck y'all Elmer Fudd-lookin, 'Humpty Dumpty ass, racist motherfuckers!" someone shouted. The bus had quieted a bit when the officers got on, but because of the humiliation, cats took up their horns, djembes, gongs, and started jamming and screaming. Earl Freeman got off the bus and started beating it with his bullwhip, all the time cursing and shouting about unfair white folks. I mean, motherfuckers was dancing in the aisle, standing on seats. The German girls was so turned on they started three-way kissing, themselves and one of the cats. Three tongues inter-swerving. The marijuana fumes filled the air; the customs officials didn't have a moment to address that. After their protests and demands for silence were ignored, they decided to get off the bus. About five minutes later, the BYG tour manager, seemingly quite shaken, got back on the bus and told the driver, who was also visibly shaken, that we could proceed. After Earl Freeman got done whipping the bus, it was onward to Amougies. What followed was gleeful cursing, celebration of not yielding to the colonial-minded Belgian officials, and anticipation of seriously playing the festival.

Had they wanted to, they could have denied you entry into country. That happened a lot. They could have strip-searched everybody. They could have detained you. Seems you got off real easy.

The festival was important for Belgium, and there was some serious local money behind it. And so, as it goes, money talks. And for certain, BYG's man on the bus did whatever had to be done to ensure that we got into the country.

How did it go from there?

Outside of a performing with the Art Ensemble, Louis Moholo, Frank Zappa and others, my main focus was on Linda, who by this time, I was totally in love with. I don't like crowds, so that aspect of the festival offered no appeal to me. I was only present for the performances I was involved with, or back stage if there was someone I wanted to see. So yeah, it was about spending time with Linda. By the time the festival was over, we had sealed the deal. From then onward we were an item. Inseparable—for a time.

It seems now you are in the groove, on the scene, living the life.

Yeah, that's right. Living it. The day-to-day was a steady groove. Gigs, dinners, parties, music, and projects. In fact, one theatre project comes to mind. I was approached by a lady by the name of Tria French to audition for a part in a play written and directed by the highly-acclaimed Antoine Bourseiller. I suggest our readers who have interest in cinema, theatre, opera, and directing to research the life and work of Bourseiller. I think he made mistake with one of his choices. That was the play, *Oh! America!* Briefly, among other issues, it dealt with America's political and racial turmoil, as perceived by, in part, Eldridge Cleaver. The rhythm and lives of black people were totally homogenized in the production. The music, composed by a white American Carl Hauser, was an insult to the black experience. And when I reflect on those days, I find it hard not to believe that was deliberate. Deliberate because he and some of his band, who were once a garage band called The Druids of Stonehenge, were clueless about the black struggle in America. Yeah, they liked R&B, and covered tunes by Bo Diddley and Screaming Jay Hawkins, like many others have. But what they knew about Cleaver and the Black Panthers was what they heard on the news, if they even listened. Carl Hauser further insulted the movement by being boundlessly arrogant in his interactions with the people of color in the theatre group. Bourseiller in this instance was simple-minded, or at the very least, in-credibly naive. How can you use punk-ass musicians, with no kinship or affinity for the struggles of black people, to provide a musical backdrop for their struggles? I think that he should have acquired the services of a black composer–maybe an understudy of the likes of Quincy Jones. Us Blacks in the group, and some French actors and critics, thought this to be a slap in the face to black culture. In fact, at a performance at the Odeon in Paris, one of the actors read a scathing review from a popular newspaper rather than saying his lines. Terrible. The show was well received in Marseilles, where the audience was more provincial and under-exposed, but in Cosmopolitan Paris, it was a complete flop. The Paris public had a steady diet of good theater for years, including work by Boursellier. Because *Hair* was a huge success in Paris, I believe Bourseiller thought *Oh!America!* had the same potential. But you know, the Paris music scene had been and was home to some of the greatest musicians of all time. Then Bourseiller shows up with Carl Hauser's soulless band to play before a well-seasoned audience. It didn't work. The question was why? With all the great black musicians who were in Paris at that time...why? I understand for Hauser and his boys, it was a gig—a well-paying gig. Outside of *the Oh! America!* flop, there are probably no other blemishes that ugly on Boursellier's career, nor Hauser's for that matter. Doing Druids music, I'm certain he was superb. I understand he has become a remarkably skilled and important doctor in Boston. Bravo.

Do you regret having participated?

Not at all. It was a valuable experience. I learned a lot every day: how to follow instructions of the director, how rehearsals are organized into segments, how to work with choreographers, technicians, and other key personnel needed to bring a production into being. The whole experience was exciting and highly beneficial to me as an artist. Also, I was bound by contract. If I had wanted to quit, I couldn't, legally. The problems I mentioned were frustrating for sure. On the other hand, I'm glad I had the opportunity to work with Antoine Bourseiller, and I worked with some extraordinary, talented people who were in the play. The great sister and brother music team, Catherine and Maxime La Forestier, and Samurai martial arts actors who taught me exercises that I use to this day.

And here's a quick digression for you. I met the great Mauritanian actor and director Med Hondo. Fast forward to 1986. I'm walking down Michigan Avenue in Chicago past the Fine Arts Theater, and I see a poster for the Blacklight Film Festival, featuring the films of Med Hondo, and he is also the guest speaker. Unbelievable. I contacted the info number on the poster and reached the festival director, Floyd Webb. I told Floyd about working with Med in France, and boom! We all hooked up. And so, as things go in the cosmos, because of Bourseiller, I met Med and Floyd, and Floyd and I have collaborated on a few projects over the years. Floyd and I have been friends ever since then.

When was the play finally over?

The whole ordeal was around ten months. The last bit, from November '70, to January '71, being in Paris. And when it was over, I was ready for a change. By this time Linda and I were full Paris residents. We were also starting to have more and more disagreements. She'd go back to Toronto maybe for a month. Then we'd patch things up and she would return to Paris. I was playing lots of gigs, many with Memphis Slim, and some with the Ron Altbach and the King

Harvest Boys. When Linda and I were together we also spent a lot of time in London with a friend named Raynes Knapp, who we initially met at a gig I was playing with Memphis Slim at the Trois Mailletz in Paris. Raynes and Julio eventually hubbed up– you know, briefly. She is a lovely person who wrote an interesting and informative book called *Bombers and Mash: The Domestic Front 1939-1945*. It's an insight into the rigors of being a mother and a woman during the war years in England. It has great photos, recipes, and recollections. Readers, check it out, authored by Raynes Minns, her married name.

I gather you were trying to expand beyond Paris?

Indeed. You see, the last thing I wanted to do was to become a fixture on the scene. When we first got there in sixty-nine, the cats were a novelty on the scene. But it was important to call your own shots, be in control of how you are perceived. My thing was to vanish from the scene for lengthy periods, like six months or so, but keep in touch with key people.

What did you do during some of those absences?

After Julio cut his album, *Rainbows All Over My Blues*, out at Herouville Studios near Paris, we decided get out of town for a few. We mixed the album in London at Olympia studios; that provided a few weeks of relief from the rigors of Paris. On that trip Linda and I rented a flat in Hampstead on South Hill Park, just off the Hampstead Heath. For the next couple of months, we enjoyed travelling around the U.K., enjoying the party scenes in Chelsea, Mayfair, Hampstead, and other areas. Also, during that period, through a lady friend, a well-known socialite who wants to remain anonymous, Julio and I met Christopher MacLehose, who at the time was an editor at Barrie & Jenkins Press, London. Julio and I proposed a collection of poetry to be titled *South Side Poets*. It was to consist of contributions from the jazz and blues communities in Chicago and the Paris transplants. Contract was signed, book was created, edited, and ready for press. Then the decision makers decided it was just too radical for British audiences. Plus, the poetry editor totally ruined the language of the streets, of jazz, of voodoo, and of raw soul. That was our first publishing/editing endeavor. MacLehose years later founded MacLehose Press, which has had some hits including *The Girl with the Dragon Tattoo*.

I was hoping that after Julio finished his album that we would go on the road to promote it. Not to be. He opted to go to Greece instead and relax. I was against this. What's the point having a record deal, then not promoting your work? Truthfully though, on the road with him would have been difficult. He was too much of an individualist, too self-centered, to be an effective band leader. It's necessary to look after the needs of the people who look up to you if one desires to lead. Sometimes you must share their burdens and display empathic concern. He didn't have that type of patience then. Maybe now he does. Since we weren't going to be working, we decided to meet in Corfu, Greece in July of seventy-one. We went our separate ways for a few months.

Did you and Linda stay on in London a bit longer?

We were in and out, back and forth to Paris, as Linda was getting modeling work in both cities. Eventually, we went to Paris and lived in a flat near the Tour Eiffel, on Avenue Charles Floquet. It was the residence of a friend, Cathy, who was a real close friend of *Jet Magazine* columnist and Jazzman, Art Simmons. Cathy's dinner parties were an exceptional mixture of Paris life: diplomats, musicians, literati, and socialites. Living with her was big fun, and certainly of great benefit socially. Yeah, that was all good for a time. Then, as things can go in this world, I introduced Cathy to Steven, a sax player. Shit, they fell in love after knowing each other about a week. Linda and I were out of a crib. Steven convinced her that his love was so fucking overwhelming that he couldn't bear to have anyone else around. Bullshit. He needed a place to flop, and Cathy wanted a man.

What did y'all do?

In a way, the situation was a blessing. I had a great friend, Moya Hayden, whose mother was quite fond of me. During one of the many break-ups Linda and I had, Moya and I managed a slight fling. Her mother, for whatever reason, wanted to see us together. She went as far as to bring me to the family horse ranch in Arras, Normandy. But Moya resisted, got drunk and silly as a tool to repulse, and that probably was the best thing that could have happened. No new entanglements were needed at that time. Anyway, her mom was closely associated with management of the France et Choiseul hotel on Rue Sainte-Honore, just off Place Vendôme. Let me add here that the hotel and restaurant are now called Hotel Costes, and it's one of the heppest hotel and cafe scenes in Paris. Linda and I resided at the France and Choiseul for about two weeks before I began a string of gigs, as the Chicago Beau Blues Band, on the Côte d'Azur, starting with a club called the Boîte de Valbonne.

Now here's a funny thing about irony and the Cosmics. Steven was the reason Linda and I had to move into the France et Choiseul. Now dig this. I wanted a background singer-dancer on the gigs, so I went and checked out Bobbi, an Australian woman that I knew was looking for an opportunity to perform. I didn't know her well; I just had a couple of chats with her at the restaurant of the American Centre, where she had a job waiting tables. I was eating there one day and mentioned the upcoming gigs and asked her if she'd like to give it a try. Man, she welcomed the opportunity. She was excited and ready to rehearse, get serious. I gave Bobbi the details of the gig travel arrangements, etcetera. We would be taking the Mistral overnight train, then I would rent a car for the trips along the coast. Bobbi suggested that maybe we would all be more comfortable driving all the way. I didn't have a car, and told her, nice idea, but that was not a possibility. And as pointed and matter of fact as a person can be, Bobbi said, "I'll buy you a car." I didn't doubt that she was serious, I just thought, what an extraordinary person. Bobbi was waitressing, but she was by no means poor. That very same afternoon, Bobbi and I went to a cabine telèphone at the post office where she called her father and asked him to sell several thousands of dollars of mining stock that she owned. Boom! Three days later we went to American Express together where Bobbi received $15,000; she put $10,000, around 50,000 Francs, in my hand. I went car shopping and ended up buying a red Ford Taunus station wagon, perfect for the band's needs.

Just like that, your situation changed. You're going to drive, not dealing with equipment and baggage on the train. Not lugging stuff around train stations and relying on cabs or somebody to pick you up.

Exactly. The kindness and huge soul of one woman had a lasting impact. Here is an ironic and funny bit that happened. On the way to southern France, I had to make a stop at the American Centre on Boulevard Raspail to pick up François, a truly gifted guitarist from Senegal, and Bobbi. I parked right in front of the entrance, and Steven happened to be hanging around. Steven asked me about my car. I told him that I just bought it to do some upcoming gigs. Now here's something I did not know. Steven and Bobbi once had a thing going on. During our light chit chat, I asked who was inside, who was hanging out. He said that Bobbi was inside. I said something like, she is a nice lady. He said, "Oh man, you like her, you can have her. I had that; she ain't about nothing." He said they had done a thing for a minute, and suggested that if I wanted her, go for it. But me and Bobbi had no physical attraction. And that's probably why we were able to deal, you dig—none of the challenges of deep involvement.

Bobbi and François came out together. They were cheerful and excited about the trip. Steven acted surprised to see that Bobbi was part of the band. Anyway, Bobbi, François, and Steven exchanged greetings. Once they were in the car, Steven was going on about Bobbi being an ex that he had to cut loose. I told him that I thought she was special. His exact words were: "She special, huh. Well, like I said, you got that." I was saying good-bye to Steven when he suddenly asked me about the car again. He asked how much it cost. The price was around $6,500. Steven said: "Damn man, how did you manage that?" I sort of lied. I said I had some money left from recordings, and that a couple of band members had chipped in. Then I just couldn't help putting it on the man who put me out of my home and spoke so badly about Bobbi. "Yeah, people chipped in, but Bobbi donated $5000," I said. What followed was an instant Negro Meltdown. I soon as I said $5,000, Steven started gasping, shaking, then he screamed, "That bitch gave you $5,000!" "Why yes. Certainly, you approve. Helping out the cause right? But none of that should matter as you don't like her anyway, right? You've been standing here telling me that she ain't about shit." Steven walked up the street and stood on a park bench and vomited. Yes, he just stood there vomiting. I shouted to him, asking if he was okay. He said he was. Then I got in the car and started driving to the Riviera. **That's an amazing twist of fate. The person Steven basically dis-**

missed as a nobody helped you and herself. And poor Steven, it seems, was consumed by his own greed and meanness, then shocked that it would come back on him like a slap across the face.

Yeah man, you know. I was trying to help him out by introducing him to Cathy, as she had lots of contacts and a social scene outside of the usual musicians' crowd. He was up until that point a pretty decent fellow. But I think when he saw Cathy's set-up, he let greed swallow him up, spit him out. Of course, after this happened we rarely spoke. But I don't think he's a bad person, not at all. Some cats just need a lesson; we all do from time to time. He had a ton of fans in France, and a person who loved his music bequeathed him a lovely condominium near the center of Paris.

How was the trip south?

Fun. There were five of us in the car just having a good time—singing, stopping for food and drink, and just enjoying the ride. It was Marva Broome, Francois, Bobbi, and Little Bill, the drummer. Jimmy Jones, a bassist, met us at the club in Valbonne. Everything went well with the gig. But in Nice the car broke down, and it was the weekend– no way to get it fixed. It was three days before our next gig. This was a real drag because the car wasn't moving. I decided to send anyone to Paris by train who wanted to go. I had to cancel two gigs which I rebooked later. Everybody wanted to go back. After I paid everybody from the Valbonne gig, and the train fares, I had about 1,000 Francs in my pocket. Maybe that was enough to fix the car, maybe not. I heard my gambling ancestors calling my name. Just like back in New York. After everyone was on the train, I strolled from the train station to the Casino Municipale de Nice. I decided to play Boule, a game similar to Roulette, with better odds for the player but less of a payout. Eleven-to-one is the payout. I walked in willing to wager 500 Francs. I walked out with 5,000 Francs. It took about an hour. I was saved. Found a decent little hotel, got the car fixed on Monday morning. It was an electrical problem, cost around 1,000 Francs to fix. Wednesday morning, I was back in Paris, with some money in my pocket.

Hang with Cosmics, your things are going to work out.

That's right. And I had a great time, even with the car problems. I met some nice people in the casino, who I still know today. On the way back I stopped in a small town, Alba la Romaine, for a quick squirm with a good friend, Irene. That was the right thing to do because the last time I'd been with her in Paris, I had consumed too much red wine to make anything happen.

Where was Linda during this time?

Linda had gone to visit Raynes in London, then she was heading to Toronto to wait until she heard from me to see what our next move would be.

And what was the next move?

As I've said: I thought it a good idea to sometimes be off the Paris scene. Now that I had a car, and a little money, with more money coming in from session work, I decided to head back to the South of France and then to Italy. Linda and I would meet in Nice, then drive up to Tourette-sur-Loup to visit our friend poet Hart Leroy Bibbs, and on the going back, pop in on James Baldwin, who lived in Sainte-Paul de Vence, which is closer to Nice. We had our rendezvous in mid-April. I picked up Linda from the airport in Nice. It was a fun time: great restaurants, beautiful spring scenery in the Maritime Alps, the stimulating company of Leroy Bibbs and his lady Jacqueline, and our daughter Jessica was conceived at Chez Bibbs et Jackie. Linda's visit was short. I don't remember why, but suddenly she had to return to Toronto. Maybe she sensed her pregnancy and wanted to be checked out. Or maybe she missed her family. Anyway, I didn't like that she was leaving; she had just arrived. We agreed to meet in Rome in June.

You head to Rome, and Linda to Toronto?

I took Linda to the Côte d'Azur airport, and I drove to Rome where fun was waiting.

Hilton Nordica
Reykjavik Blues Festival, Reykjavik, Iceland
19-21 March, 2016

Here we are for your concert here in Iceland, and perhaps the final interviews for book one. Are you ready?
 Ready for everything. Music, fun, time with family and hanging with you to get this work completed.
Rome?
 Yes, Roma! I headed to Rome in my red Ford station wagon. One of the first things I did when I arrived was to look up James Peter Outlaw, an acquaintance I had made on a previous trip. Peter was a Philadelphia transplant who had come to Rome looking for acting jobs during the Italian filmmaking boom. He was one of the very few Blacks on the scene that included Harold Bradley, founder of the internationally renowned Folk Studio in Trastevere, and former Minnesota Vikings football star; Woody Strode, who was known for his role in *Spartacus*; and Gospel singer, Jho Jenkins. Italian-made Westerns were big during this time. In the cafes along the Via Veneto, like Harry's Bar and Cafe de Paris, one could nearly always run into film people like Claudia Cardinale, Clint Eastwood, Marcello Mastroianni, Federico Fellini, Sergio Leone, Henry Fonda, and all kinds of artists, fans, people from the press, just hanging out–having four-hour lunches then staggering to a taxi to go home and sleep before the lengthy evening dinner sessions. And in the evening, certain parts of Rome were an unending promenade. Where can one end up? Never can tell. In the Hotel Excelsior, just off Via Veneto, Jazzman Tony Scott had a club. It was swinging. I ran into Gore Vidal in there one night, who later introduced me to Giorgio Bassani, who loved jazz. I'll tell you about Giorgio in a minute.
I know you always contemplate your position, so how did you position yourself in Rome?
 Well, in the beginning I was at the mercy of Peter Outlaw to introduce me around. Peter was well known and generally liked. He was viewed by many as an eccentric. Most of his clothes were custom made. He drove an Alfa Romeo 1750, a nice sports car, and he and his lady Ochie had a nice home at Via Latina Malabranca 15, in

the Aventino district. Ochie's family had precious metals holdings in some country in southern Africa. She was German so maybe it was Namibia. Once a month Ochie would travel to Africa to see her family. After a week, she would return to Rome, and Peter would have access to around $20,000, which he would begin spending immediately. In the days while Ochie was away, he was usually broke, so he pawned jewelry and other valuables to get by until she returned. I remember once Peter had a white suit made with gold stitching on the cuffs and collars. It was ridiculous looking. Anyway, when the suit was completed he took it to a jeweler to verify if the tailor had used thread that contained real gold. It didn't, and Peter went off on the tailor. The tailor explained to Peter, as had the jeweler, that real gold would flake off the thread after the suit was worn one or two times. Peter said he would buy another one. I knew then that this was a fool with his money. Like I said, Peter was my guide for a while. He did some good things like helping establish house accounts at cafes, tailors, and other useful businesses. He introduced me to the high-end gambling crowd that met in various private clubs around Rome. For a while I was a regular at craps and Black Jack games.

Back to your question: How did I position myself? For one thing, not as Chicago Beau or Lincoln Beauchamp. In Peter's circles, I was known as D'Tiribias. I knew that period in Rome would be a short one, and I also wanted to experiment with living out a literary fantasy that I was creating as I went along.

How did you come up with D'Tiribias?

The word just popped into my mind. Maybe I was recalling something I'd read in a novel or heard spoken. Sounds Brazilian or Portuguese. Anyway, D'Tiribias is who I was as I moved around with Peter and Ochie. At the clubs and discos like Numero Uno and Scarabocchio, the gaming tables in Ostia, the private villas along the road the Viterbo, and at the countless parties in Rome, I was D'Tiribias. When asked about the origins of my name, I said that I was named after great-grandparent who lived in Bahía. I never gave a surname.

Man, I know you were having a great time in Italy. And I sat with you in Piazza Navona. It was remarkable the number of beautiful women who were just out shopping and walking about.

I mean, stunning ladies everywhere.

LaBosse, I was twenty-two years old. I was hanging with ladies that were my age down to eighteen, and I had some lady friends up into their forties and fifties. Rome attracts beautiful women and men from around the world. And I'm not talking about just what's considered by many to be physical beauty, that's one thing, which is unfortunately biased; I'm talking state-of mind. The weather, fashion, lifestyle, cuisine, international scene are all conducive to sex, romance, sensory stimulation... just feeling alive! I can stand at the top of the Spanish Steps, or in Villa Panfili, or Monte Verde, or stroll the marketplace on Ettore Rolli, laughing with Romani friends; I'm surrounded by beauty. By humanity that exists in beauty. No place is perfect, but beauty is a plus no matter what type. **Italy is a very family-oriented society, right? How did this affect your sometimes-lascivious behavior?**

Undoubtedly, there are complications, especially in the roles of women that are usually, and unfortunately, dictated by tired-ass, hypocritical men. You have many people who live outside of so-called traditions, because they feel that they are flawed and they may feel trapped. Others live outside for awhile, then go back to keep peace within their families. Many know the truth about virtue, especially in Catholic tradition, and Rome, being the seat of this nonsense, is loaded with closet doubters. And many have experienced the ubiquitous hypocrisy firsthand, as I have. And let me say this while I'm thinking about it: I knew priests, nuns, bishops, and other figures in Rome who were more decadent than I could have ever imagined. I knew some that had families, mistresses, and gambling, alcohol, sex, and drug addictions. Others were exactly as is being exposed today. And some were quite open with their behavior. You know, everything has an inside and an outside. Religion is no different. You have the insiders who run things and do what they want, and the outsiders who choose to believe what they are told, and the insiders profit immensely.

I moved around in circles that could be considered hep. My girlfriends were living outside of the usual traditions in a way. I mean, one doesn't necessarily have to completely reject tradition to push the boundaries. I knew several women that knew they had to be virgins when they married. And they preserved their virginity for their future husbands. However, that didn't stop them from being active and creative sexually. As one good lady friend told me, her every orifice was mine to explore, but penetration of her vagina was off limits. If she was not a virgin on her wedding night, she would be ruined in more ways than I could imagine. Well, I certainly was fine with that. Just fine! And over the course of time I've known ladies in different parts of the world who were bound to the same tradition of virginity, who, if for no other reason than to preserve their sanity and fulfill needs, sought alternatives. And really, this is fucked up, hypocritical, male thinking. Basically, the same shit that's got the planet fucked up.

And again, as to my behavior, I also knew many ladies who were visiting Italy. One of the most fun was a lady by the name of Carla, who claimed to be heiress to a bubble gum company. She was an American woman of about 25 years; I don't remember where she was from. She would be referred today as a plus-size lady. She was stunningly beautiful, and the Italians, unlike Americans at the time, also thought she was beautiful. Rubenesque and then some. Yeah!

You were going to tell me something Gore Vidal and Giorgio Bassani?

Ah yes. Clarinet player Tony Scott had a jazz club in the Excelsior Hotel. I was in there one night just hanging and recognized Gore sitting with a couple of people. It wasn't surprising to see him in Tony Scott's as Tony was a big name in jazz. He was on top of the *Playboy* Jazz Poll, which, as contrived as it was, gave Tony Scott a lot of recognition among certain people. Tony had worked with some of the greats, and beyond a doubt he was one of the few cats who specialized only in the clarinet. But he was arrogant with a horrible temper. Honestly, I didn't want to go to jail, that's the only reason I didn't kick his ass on several occasions, because he could get loud and rude in your face. It was as though he thought that because he spent a lot of time around black people that he earned the privilege to disrespect us if he happened to be in a bad mood. But really, he didn't know how close he came to getting a thorough blues-inspired ass-whuppin.

Anyway, on this evening I found a seat near the Vidal group.

I was thinking of ways to cut into the conversation going on at his table without being rude, and certainly I didn't want to be rebuked. I decided to edit a line from Albert Camus' *The Fall*. I went to the bar, and as I returned to my seat, I was hoping that the timing would be right for me to approach the Vidal party. It was. I approached and said, "May I, signori Vidal, without running the risk of intruding, introduce myself to you, with the hope that you and your friends here will not admonish me for my boldness?" Vidal laughed and said, "Straight out of Camus with a twist." He stood up, I introduced myself, we shook hands, and I was invited to join his table. We chatted about music, writing, Roma, but mostly listened to music. Vidal thought it interesting that a 22-year-oldblack man from Chicago who had introduced himself via Camus was sitting at his table in Roma– and that we were comfortably enjoying the evening, conversation, and the pleasure of the coming together from entirely different cultures through the power of music, literature, and mutual cultural admiration. There were many people in the club. Over the next hour several people stopped by the table and said hello. And there were other well-known people in the club as well. It was that type of scene. I asked Vidal if he knew writer Giorgio Bassani, who I knew had a great interest in jazz. He said he could put me in touch with him. We exchanged phone numbers, and the next day, he called me and said he had spoken with Bassani, and that he had given the okay for me to have his phone number. Amazing. Vidal and Bassini in a twenty-four-hour span.

Did you introduce yourself to Gore Vidal as Beauchamp?

Absolutely. D'Tiribias was mostly used in introductions from Peter. There was a whole other channel working in my head for other matters.

Were you surprised that Vidal got back with you so quickly?

I was, and that was an amusing situation. Here's why: I was living in the Pensione Daria on Via Sicilia near Via Veneto– a perfect location at the time. My room in the pensione had a phone, but it wasn't working. When I got the call from Vidal, the phone was answered by the daughter of the owner. It was a family-owned business. Man, she ran down the hall to my room shouting, "Signori Beau, Signori Beau, Signori Vidal al telefono per te!" Everybody who was in the ristorante heard her. English and Americans murmured, "Huh, wow, Gore Vidal!" I went to the phone. Gore could hear the commotion through the phone. When I picked up the receiver I could hear him laughing. I explained that I couldn't speak as I wished because the phone in my room was broken. No matter, we chatted briefly, and he gave me Giorgio Bassani's phone number. After that call we were never in touch again. A few years later, music impresario Isio Saba had arranged concerts for me in Ravello, near the Amalfi coast. I caught a glimpse of Vidal from the stage. He nodded and gestured a slight wave. When my set was done, he was gone. That's the last time I saw him.

Interesting the way this is playing out. When you went to Rome you wanted to meet Bassini, but you never thought that would come about because of a chance meeting with Gore Vidal. Is that right?

Yes. The Cosmics will work with you if you let them. And Vidal– he was cool, elegant; I am truly appreciative to have had a bit of time with him. I mean, Vidal was the quintessential disdainer of the American political system. Back then, we had some things in common, like the dislike for Norman Mailer's writing. And recently, he made the statement that Barack Obama is too intelligent for the American public. He could be right. We'll see. I was reminding myself back then saying, "I ain't but twenty-two years old. What great good fortune!"

For sure, Beau. For sure. And now, Giorgio Bassani.

I rang Bassani, and of course he was expecting to hear from me. We arranged to meet at his home in Rome. As I remember, his place was quite large, with the items around one would expect from a writer and lover of the arts. I wasn't sure if this was his main residence, or maybe a place he used possibly for reclusive or creative purposes. He had a sizable collection of LPs, and a state-of-the-art stereo system; Charles Mingus could be heard over the speakers as we sat in a kind of drawing room. And he was curious as to why a young black man from the South Side of Chicago had interest in his work. I explained that even as a child I felt a closeness to things past, not only in my own culture, but also the cultures of others. But also, to be connected to history through books and meeting people who

had certain experiences were of great importance to me. I told him about the Jews who came to my concerts in France, and how some said the first black people they had ever seen were soldiers liberating them from the Nazi death camps of Poland and Germany. I told him how many had come to love the culture of their liberators through jazz, blues, and other elements of the culture of black people. I explained that I had never witnessed white people so moved by anything black people did in the United States. Bassani was visibly moved as I related what had been told to me by the former death camp prisoners. He said that under Mussolini, things had deteriorated rapidly for Italian Jews. Name changing and living undercover back during the war years was a part of everyday life for him, his family, and nearly their entire community in Ferrara. He mentioned his time in prison, and his time writing and working under a different name, Giacomo Marchi, to avoid being recognized as a Jew. I told him a few black people had used that option because they were extremely light skinned and could pass for white. Many of the "passers" felt they had betrayed their race by hiding amongst the enemy during exceedingly tough times. And many were at the forefront, and also working behind the scenes, from the Underground Railroad to the Civil Rights Movement. Bassani was well informed, and even though he was from a well-to-do family of physicians and educators, he completely understood the nature of struggle, and he completely understood the global danger of Aryanism as extolled by Hitler and spineless Mussolini. We spoke about jazz, blues, and other music and artists like Django Reinhardt, Billie Holiday, John Coltrane, McCoy Tyner, Memphis Slim, Count Basie, Duke Ellington, Josephine Baker, and others. Bassani played piano, mostly European genres, but he also had a love for jazz that he pursued on piano only for personal pleasure, he said.
Did you speak much about his writings?

Very little. I was there because I admired *The Garden of The Finzi-Continis*, and his word-smithing genius. I knew that I was not a literary peer by any means, nor did I want to take up his time in a discussion about his work like some arrogant, inexperienced student attempting to critique rather than learn. Bassani had children my age. One son was born in 1949, the same year as I. I was there out of respect and admiration, and at the most, wanted to share experiences, as my parents and black people had experiences, like with the Jews, in dealing with Aryan supremacy that were not dissimilar.

How long was your visit?

About an hour. And I was grateful for that much time. He was impressed that I was a young Bluesman, and thought, correctly, that black culture would be underrepresented in jazz and blues if young people did not carry the flame. Bassani had been Vice-president of RAI, the Italian state radio and television station. He was connected with all things cultural in Italy. He asked me if I would be interested in performing on Italian television, and of course I said yes.

Our meeting was entering the wind-down phase. Bassani indicated that he had other meetings that afternoon, and I suggested that maybe I should not be taking so much of his time. It was a cool, mutual desire to bring things to a close. Before I left, Bassani asked me to hang on a moment while he disappeared into another room. My curiosity was momentary as he emerged from that room and handed me a sealed envelope that was addressed to someone at RAI Television. There was also a phone number of his contact written on the envelope. He advised me to call and make an appointment, and said he would advise the person that I would be getting in touch. And with that we said good-bye. I thanked him for his time, and he told me that he was honored that he had an admirer from the Land of *il Blues*. He wished me well, and I left.

What a remarkable visit. Did you ever meet again?

No, we did not. I knew we wouldn't, at least not soon. Maybe down the line a few years, but that never happened. This is the thing about some fine people who happen to be great: they make time for you, but one must remember that their time is precious. I respect people's time. I knew he had a huge agenda, and a life to live, as did I.

Dig it.

About three days after our meeting, I called the number on the envelope and reached the gentleman to whom I was being referred. We set up a meeting at RAI a few days later. I don't remember the gentleman's name, but I think he held the position of Vice-president at the station, as Bassani once had. I gave him the envelope which contained a letter of introduction. I also gave him recordings that I had done with Archie Shepp. We spoke about the appreciation of jazz and blues in Italy, which was quite broad. Many towns, from Palermo to Bolzano, held festivals that invited artists, both well-known and unknown. He told me that there may be an opportunity for me to appear on Italian television at some point, but he couldn't say when. My host asked me if I minded waiting a few minutes while he left the office for a few minutes.

Did you find that strange?

I did, since he was gone about 20 minutes. When he came back he was apologetic for taking so long. Then he handed me an envelope and said that something unexpected had come up and that he would have to end our meeting. We agreed to stay in touch. I told him that I was not sure about where I would be in Rome in the coming weeks but I would let him know. And with that the meeting ended.

And did you keep in touch?

I did not because things were happening at an extremely rapid pace. Also, he had said something may be arranged down the road, and I knew at the pace I was moving, there was no way I could predict my own movements. I was twenty-two and on the move. Having big fun and lots of lady friends. I was occasionally gambling and running with Peter Outlaw. I mean I focused on important matters. I took my intellectual pursuits seriously. Meeting Bassani was a priority. Stability was not. In fact, I hated the word.

What about the envelope?

Oh, yes. I got a real surprise. I opened the envelope as I sat in a taxi riding back to Via Veneto. It contained a handwritten note that said basically: "Welcome to Roma. Giorgio Bassani has asked that I help you in any way possible in advancing your music career here in Italy. Hopefully, one day we may be able to present you on RAI Television, but I cannot confirm when. Please accept the enclosed soldi to help you along with your young career. Sincerely...".

The envelope contained 1,000 U.S.

How generous!

Man, I was floored. Bassani must have been impressed with me, and I know for sure he felt deep empathy for, and could relate to, the struggles of black Americans—and the ingratitude of the American people and politicians for the service of Blacks in both wars. He was very aware of the lynchings of World War One and World War Two vets and the civil rights struggle. And on behalf of Jews liberated from the camps, he expressed his gratitude to black soldiers. I think for Bassani, helping me was an essential act– an opportunity that he welcomed. You know, sometimes a situation pops up that gives you a chance to do a good deed that's been in your mind. Bassani saw a chance to do good, and being a good person, he did so.

Yeah, man. And one should not ignore those opportunities. The Cosmics set it up for us act on. It happens both ways: to give and to receive. Next move?

I heard from Linda. She was coming to Rome in a week so that meant I had a lot to organize—in terms of lady friends, some solutions. One of them, an Australian beauty Andrea, was also living in the Pensione Daria. At some point, we had agreed to travel together to Greece, now I had to figure a way out of that promise. She knew nothing of Linda, which was probably a mistake. I should have told her to spare ill feelings. So, I eventually told her that Linda was coming and that we were trying to patch things up for the umpteenth time. And she said she was cool with that, and that she would go to Greece alone, and let's keep in touch. Back then that was not easy when people were on the move. We'd write letters to each other in care of Poste Restante and hope they'd be received. That's what Andrea and I agreed to do.

Over the next week I became scarce with the ladies except for Andrea, as she was my down-the-hall neighbor. And man, you know, we had a special kind of thing going on, no intercourse. But not like the women who were saving themselves. She was wired differently. She was strictly an *oralista*, in every sense, and I was navigating through old taboos, becoming an *oralisto*. Ha-ha! Salad tossing was her specialty, and I soon developed a fondness for the art as both recipient and administrator.

I should point out that like many young men, especially where I came from, thought that they were knowledgeable about matters of sex and romance. Most of us were extremely misinformed. Generally, the perpetrators of sexual myths and out-and-out lies were the older cats and ladies. And there were taboos regarding nearly everything outside of straight up-and-down missionary sex. Once, when I was around seventeen, back in Chicago, I laid my head in my girlfriend's lap as we sat on the sofa. I raised her skirt, and began kissing her inner thigh, slowing moving towards her vagina. As I kissed her there, panties still on, she shouted, "Please don't degrade yourself! Please don't!" I sat up and asked her why that would be degrading. Her answer reflected the same taboos and myths I had heard from older guys. She rambled on about that being something only bull daggers and bitches in jail did. But when it came to fucking, we did that every chance we got. This is a quick reflection on one sex taboo where I grew up. Of course, the hookers and so-called hoes did it all. Ah! I wanna be with the degraded, all the way down to no grade. Grade zero!

Ha-ha! I hear you. You were getting an education?

Exactly. Not only from Andrea, but others. And when I think about those ignorant ass, shit-talking motherfuckers back where I grew up, I hope they have expanded at least a little bit. But I do know that a lot that talk was also hypocrisy. You know people talk in a neighborhood, around the pool rooms, beauty shops, barber shops, chicken shacks, etcetera. Everybody was fucking, but nobody wanted to have a reputation as a pussy-eater or a dick-sucker. And I could go on about the many closet gay people. I'll save that for another time. But they did struggle, and thank goodness times have changed for the better.

Let's go back to Roma.

Right. Linda came to Rome earlier than expected. She rang from Toronto and said she was arriving the next day. That was two days before Andrea was heading to Greece. Now Linda, she made her presence known. For one thing, she wore about twenty bracelets that could be heard rattling from thirty feet away. She was and is beautiful, and her arrival was noticed by all who happened to be about in the pensione, including Andrea. The following morning after Linda's arrival, Andrea knocked at my door, which had now become Linda's door as well. Linda opened the door. Andrea asked for me, and Linda, of course, asked her who was she. She replied that she was a friend staying in the pensione, was leaving, and had dropped by to say goodbye. I introduced Linda and Andrea, then I stepped out into the hall with her for a private chat. Linda went back in but left the door ajar to eavesdrop. However, she forgot that whenever she moved she clanked like a bucket of chains, so I heard her and moved my conversation to the dining area—and at that moment I heard my room door slam shut. Uh-oh, I thought: now I have to deal with her angry ass.

You could see it coming. Drama! Right?

Yeah, man. For sure. I went back to the room and got my shoes and a jacket. I told Linda I what I was doing, which was going to Roma Termini with Andrea, and I'd be back shortly. Now, Linda wanted to have a conversation about Andrea right then and there. For what? She got suspicions based on a knock at the door and a pretty face. Andrea and I went to the train station and said our goodbyes. She was sorry to have to leave but that was best, not to be in a situation. She was right– sad and disappointed. And at that point, Linda was being her usual self that had kept us fighting for the past two years. Petty shit. Jealousy. Andrea headed to Brindisi to get the ferry to Mykonos and on to Corfu. One great hug and a kiss, and that was the last that we saw of each other. No further communication. No Poste Restante. Nothing.

When you got back to the hotel?

On the way back I decided not to argue. I mean, about what? The same old shit. In this case, there was no evidence that I had done something with Andrea. I'm living in a small pensione where there is communication between the guests. People make friends. They hangout. They drink. Linda was simply jealous. She wanted to argue. I just played it cool until she calmed down. That took about a day. After a while we hooked up with Peter and Ochie and started hanging, but my patience was wearing thin with the whole scene. I love Rome, but couldn't maneuver the way I wanted to. Also, my plan was to eventually go to Corfu, not to remain in Rome. Linda and I were driving each other crazy. I suggested she go back to Toronto and we hook up later and try again to patch things up. She didn't want to do that. I decided to split and head to Greece.

Here is a big problem when people, when couples, cannot communicate. I could never get straight answers out of Linda. A question was answered with a question, or the answer was so nebulous I didn't know what to believe. I think in some schools of thought, some women think that the way you keep a man is to keep him guessing about as much as you can. Some old-ass, battle-axe, hand-me-down, fucked-up thinking. And so, to questions like: "How are you feeling?" the answer could be: "Why do you want to know?" "Because you seem a bit pale, and I'm concerned." "Whatever it is, it's nothing that you should worry about." "So you're fine?" "Yep, I guess." And then a grunt or sigh.

How long can one carry on like that?

Not long. At least I can't. After a couple of weeks of weirdness, I decided to split. Now, in retrospect, this was wrong, maybe. I figured if I split, Linda and I would do what we usually do, which was to have some expensive marathon telephone conversations, then agree to get back together, or not. That had probably happened a half-dozen times over two years. What I didn't know was that she was pregnant, and had been since we were at LeRoy Bibbs' place in the South of France. She never said a word. Said she didn't want to say anything then, but it had been two months. It's playing games that I dislike so much. Say what's happening! And what that idiotic thinking of "keep em' guessing" does, at least in my case, is lead me to not believe most of what I'm being told. A normal conversation about pregnancy would have changed everything. I only found out that she was pregnant months later when she came to Copenhagen.

I cut out and head to Corfu, and Linda, when she realizes I ain't coming back, moves in with Peter and Ochie in Aventino. La-Bosse, had I known she was pregnant, I'm sure I would have reconsidered cutting out. Today, Linda and I agree that things could have been handled differently. But you know, youthful behavior is often governed by stubbornness, big ego, carelessness, baseless decisions, and more.

That's right. But today y'all are fine.

Yeah, we real good. Linda is a great friend, and I love her dearly. She is the mother of our daughter, Jessica, and another daughter by another marriage, Micah. We had many talks over the years about what happened. We both made mistakes. Mine were childishly stupid, but I had to learn over time. We had to forgive each other and move on. We are family.

What was your next move?

I went to Greece via train from Roma, and ferry boat from Brindisi to Corfu. This is a route that has been, and still is taken by millions– from tourists to citizens of Mediterranean countries. This is an ancient route from Italy to points south, east, and west in the region. As to be expected, the boat was packed with passengers. I paid for a comfortable lounge chair on deck and huddled down with my baggage as a pillow and footrest, then snoozed through the eight-hour overnight trip until morning when the ship docked at Corfu.

Was this your first Mediterranean crossing?

Yes, across the Mediterranean into the Ionian Sea, and it was uneventful. There was lots of drinking and partying going on, but I was too exhausted to party and drink. I needed to sleep. I needed rest. I had been on the move constantly for five years. I had the idea that Corfu could provide me with a respite for a bit– and time to think through so much that had happened. And the time and atmosphere to do some writing. That was my state of mind as I relaxed on the ferry.

Did it go like that?

Somewhat. It took a minute to get into the groove, to get my bearings and find my rhythm in a totally new environment. Things started happening as soon as the ship docked. I got off the boat and was just looking around at the scene: cafes and shops of all sorts selling souvenirs, clothing, maps, Ouzo, Metaxa, cigarettes, and more. There were others soliciting scooter rentals, villas to rent, taxi services, car rentals, you name it. There were many young men hanging around the port. I later found out that hanging around the port was an all-day activity for some young Greek men. It was the catch spot to meet women. I mean, these cats were on the case. Whatever ladies may need, these young dandies had the answer. Place to live, transportation, tour of the island, romance– they were on the case. When the ferries came in, they were waiting. I was an oddity, the only Black around, and two meters and 130 kilos. A young man approached me and introduced himself as Spiro. I later learned that if one shouted "Spiro" on a busy street, 90 percent of the men in earshot would reply, "Ney!" "Yes" in Greek. Saint Spyridon is the patron saint of Corfu, hence many are named Spiro.

This Spiro was extremely friendly and welcomed me to the Island. He offered his services to help me find accommodations, and he told me that there were two others *like me* that he knew of on the island. He was not at all offensive. I understood that on Greek Islands, Blacks are rarely seen, unless they are sailors or merchant marines on ancient trade routes, but generally, not as tourists or just there to hang out as I was.

Who were the other Blacks?

Julio Finn was one, and the other was Lucy Moll. Spiro was friends with both and hinted that he was rather close to Lucy. I told him my name, and he said that Julio had spoken about me, was expecting me, but not sure when. Spiro said Julio lived in house with a woman named Milly near a village called Perama. I knew Milly. She was a good friend from Paris, and she and Julio had an off-and-on thing going on. During that summer, Milly and I became great friends. Sadly, she passed away from cancer in San Francisco in 2006.

Spiro recommended a five-star hotel, the Kontokali Palace, where Lucy was a bartender, and where one of Richard Nixon's daughters was vacationing. I don't remember if it was Tracy or Julie. I had a little money as I had sold my Ford station wagon to an Australian fellow in Piazza di Spagna in Rome, so I agreed to a couple of nights of luxury while I looked up Julio and did some exploring. That very same afternoon I met Lucy Moll. We hit it off immediately. Lucy was African-American and German, and from the get-go, was about having some fun. She said she and Spiro were friends, but nothing romantically binding. That works for me, I thought.

How about the Nixon girl, any contact with her?

When I met Lucy, the Nixon girl was poolside, and Lucy was serving her. There were maybe two visible Secret Service guys around, and probably some others embedded around some place as well as Greek security people. But you know, those were different times back then, and I don't think there was the perception of any threat. All was pretty loose, and in retrospect, that's comforting.

Did you speak with Miss Nixon?

No, I waved-nodded a greeting, and she did the same. But you know, I didn't approach her. I wasn't interested. If I had, I don't think that would have been a problem. Lucy and I agreed to meet the next day at the hotel bar. I crashed for a few hours, then went to find Julio. I didn't have to look far, or for long, as Spiro told me that he would let Julio know that I was on the island, and he could usually be found in one of the cafés along the Esplanade in Corfu Town. I should mention here that in Corfu, there are lots of structures built by the French during their occupation. The Esplanade is a street, and square, of exceptional architectural beauty. That evening I walked up and surprised Julio seated on the terrace of the Corfu Bar.

How was it seeing him after several months?

It was great seeing him again. He was in full form, seated alone, smoking a cigar and enjoying a brandy. That mal-fal tried to act like he wasn't surprised to see me, but he was, because Spiro had not gotten to him yet. At that time Julio thought that if he was perceived as uncool, the masses would lapse into a state of shock. "What, Julio's not cool!" To not be irresponsible, he kept his emotions to minimum. He believed all eyes were on him. And eyes were on him, but not for the reasons he thought. Simply, we were oddities, figures rarely if ever seen on Corfu. That's all.

Now that y'all are reunited, what happens?

As we sat in the Corfu Bar, several people came up and spoke. Julio had already been on Corfu about a month before my arrival, so he had met quite a few people. Also, recently arrived was our friend from Paris, Milly Hurlimann, was known by some Corfuotes from previous visits. In fact, it was Milly who had encouraged us to visit Corfu. The scene was pleasant and relaxed. The cafés were flourishing and the air was buzzing with conversations in several languages.

Wasn't there a little tension in the air because of the Colonels?

Things are not always as they seem. In fact, there was truly a pleasant atmosphere on Corfu, but everybody knew that the situation was entirely different on the mainland. At the whim of the Junta, everything could change in an eye blink.

Can you give our readers a little insight into what was going on in Greece during that time?

Sure, just a bit, and that's because these types of political situations are far more complex than an outside observer could ever know. On the surface, a military junta seized power in 1967, and remained in power until November of 1973. During that time there were struggles within the military complex. And believe me, there is no way I could know the motivations behind certain events. But some things were common knowledge. The torturing of opposition politicians and others; the training of young psychopaths to become torturers; the banning of certain artists' works including those of Irene Pappas, Mikos Theodorakis, and others; the banning of usage of the letter Z in certain contexts; the banning of the Beatles; the banning of the Peace sign; the banning of mini-skirts and lots more. I knew women tourists in Athens who had been escorted by the police to a shop or their hotels to buy or change clothes. I never saw this happen on Corfu. In fact, the regime under the lead colonel, George Papadopoulos, encouraged tourism, especially from NATO countries. And surely, the U.S. and Great Britain knew exactly what was happening in Greece. Typically, though, mounting reports of atrocities was met with silence from the world power supporters. The King, Constantine II, who seemed almost childlike as he was portrayed in the press, struggled with the Junta, and eventually tried his own coup that failed. But as I said, what was happening was far too intricate to fully understand. And then, why even try?

Did your Greek friends talk about what was going on?

Rarely. People didn't speak about the Junta around me. I think that was out of habit and self-preservation. There is no doubt that secret police were all around. They were in discos, at the beaches, and in tourists places. Some owned businesses and had English or American accents, as they had been educated in the U.S. or England. To be on the safe side, I never discussed politics while in Greece. Now, outside of Greece, in London, where there is a huge Greek community, I heard all kind of objections, opinions, and hypothetical plots. People said things they would never say in Greece, unless they could withstand repercussions, or able to try to make changes or support those who were.

You, Julio, and your circles kept out of politics, period?

We did. There has been a great deal written and documented about that period. All one has to do is Google. That's all. There is a lot to read, a lot to learn.

My life in Corfu was delightful. For some others, not so. Here is something that happened. I became friends with a government official named Theo, who was with the head man of the Aliens Police on Corfu and surrounding islands. Theo and I played tennis on a regular basis. Over time during our conversations off the court, he strongly hinted that the Junta turned their back on most activities by foreigners and middle-class Greeks as long as people did what they did privately. He meant using drugs, orgies, whatever. He also said that he believed that Julio and our circles of friends had been checked out, and it had been noted by the authorities that we engaged in nothing prohibited, neither privately or in public. However, there were some Americans who had become too bold with their behavior. He mentioned some people who I only slightly knew. In my travels, I rarely hung out with Americans. I mean, why travel 5,000 miles to hang out with people you just left? Reasons to travel include new people, places, and experiences.

How bold were these Americans?

Extremely bold. There were these two American sisters from Georgia, I believe. They were attractive white girls in their mid-twenties who made it obvious that they came from money and privilege. I nicknamed them the Dixie Peaches. They had a lovely villa and café near the village of Agios Giordos, which is situated on the east side of the island, quite a distance from Corfu Town. I ran into the sisters one day in town and they invited me to a party at their place. This was shortly after Theo had told about scrutiny on the island. I rented a car and went to their party. Man, these women were doing all the wrong shit in clear sight. I mean smoking grass, making transactions, half naked– all in sight. I had no intention of spending the night there. I asked one of the sisters how well she knew their guests. She said she and her sister knew some of them, but many were just cool people from the beach. I told her that I thought that she should be careful because one never knows exactly who is hanging around for whatever reasons. And to my surprise, when I mentioned the Junta, she actually knew very little. I mean, she was oblivious to what was going on in the country she was living in. Her silly arrogance was unbelievable. She resented my suggestion that they may be under scrutiny. And as it happens with in the thinking of the privileged, how dare my black ass think I can tell her anything. Arrogant and haughty, you know. Okay. This was in 1971. I learned from Greek friends in London nearly two years later that the Dixie Peaches had been arrested and had received lengthy prison sentences for possession and distribution of marijuana and other substances illegal in Greece. I warned those girls, and it was well over a year later that they got busted. And the only reason they got busted was arrogance– and a sense of white-American privilege. But more intricately, their bust coincided with dissension within the Junta. Strongman Papadopoulos was leaning toward loosening the grip on the citizens in a move he called Liberalization. His chief opponent within the Regime was hard-line, conservative, anti-communist, xenophobic, Brigadier Dimitrios Ioannidis, who eventually overthrew Papadopoulos. Ioannidis was against any reforms proposed by Papadopoulos. It was during this period that the Dixie Peaches, and others behaving as they were, ended up in jail. Fortunately, in 1974, civil rights and democracy were restored, and the colonels and their collaborators were put on trial for treason, among other charges. Some were convicted and sentenced to death. Later, the sentences were commuted to life. I heard that the Dixie Peaches were released from prison as were many others incarcerated by the Junta.

That's deep. I've seen the same thing happen over the years in other countries. But you know, you can't advise an arrogant motherfucker that wants to get high or deal. They think they can outsmart local authorities whose specialty is keeping an eye on foreigners. I mean, the Dixie Peaches were lucky for regime change.

Really. I knew people who got busted in Turkey and other countries. Not so lucky... not at all. My advice has always been: *Leave that shit alone. Drink what they drinking, that's it!*

Thanks for this recollection. Hopefully someone will read this, and if need be, take heed. Anyway, where were you living on Corfu?

Julio introduced me to Mr. Corfu. His name was Georgios Varthis, but he was all things Corfu: realtor, tour operator, travel agent: what you needed, Varthis could handle it. Varthis told me about a brand-new, never lived-in Villa at Kanoni. Varthis drove us out to have a look. The place was stunning. The exterior had typical white-washed walls. It was fully furnished with marble floors, two bedrooms, big beds, kitchen, living room with a sofa and coffee table, garden, terrace, and not far from the road. I met Demetrios Halikiopoulos, the owner, and we made a deal. The house was maybe half a kilometer from the bus turnaround, the postcard image Vlacherna Monastery, and a causeway across the bay that ran beneath the flight path of Corfu airport. If you were lucky, and your timing was right, you might get some jet fuel on you as the planes were only about two hundred feet above you at that point. Julio and Milly lived in Perama in a house called Villa Mimosa, which was about five hundred feet from the beach, directly across the sea from Albania. The causeway was convenient for going back and forth. The walk from his house to mine was about an hour. But in these kinds of places time almost has no relevance. People move slowly and schedules are not necessarily adhered to.

Moving in was easy. What you had was only baggage, right?

I went out and bought a record player. I had brought about ten of my favorite albums with me, so I was ready. The next day after renting my place, which I named Villa Advucus, the stage name of a Romani dancer friend of mine, I went to Kontokali for lunch with Lucy and asked her to move in with me, which she agreed to do without hesitation. She welcomed the change. In the beginning the arrangement was for her to have a bedroom, but I insisted that she pay nothing. All was paid in advance, and I'm the last person to nickel and dime another. If I got it, and can afford it: come and enjoy! Lucy came out to Advucus the following afternoon. She didn't come back with me the evening before because she had to explain things to Spiro, the same Spiro that had introduced us. They were having a slight affair, and it was out of respect for their friendship that she sought to put his mind at ease, or maybe ill at ease...

Our thing was platonic at that time; we'd only just met. When Lucy's taxi pulled up, the crib was ready. I had bought a stereo with four speakers—I had speakers all around the house. Curtis Mayfield's *Move on Up* was playing on the box. Every window was open. The sea breeze carried floral smells from the garden throughout the house. The breeze carried the music to neighboring villas, paths, streets. It was a utopian setting. Lucy was home.

One of those Greek Island days when everything just seems perfect. I know them well.

Indeed. There were many days like that. All day, every day, then all evening... perfection. Not as a vacation, but as a life choice. As Lucy settled in, which took only a few minutes, we both realized that the only thing that would make things more pleasant than they were would be to, without hesitation, go to bed. And that's what we did. We just got into each other and remained that way for the remainder of the summer.

In less than a week you've taken care of lots of business. You've got yourself a villa, a lady, music, a little cash, and boom– baby, you living! And on your agenda, was to...?

I wanted to reflect and write. It's 1971, and I had basically been on the road since 1966, with the exception of a few months in 1967. That's five years of adventure, travel, creating music, making mistakes, falling in and out of love, a little bit of trouble, gambling, hitchhiking, travelling first class, drinking Wild Irish Rose in the gutter, enjoying vintage Pol Roget at the Cafe de la Paix, playing on street corners for a meal, performing and recording with beacons of the Black Diaspora Experience like Archie Shepp, Philly Joe Jones, and on, and on, and on. I was convinced by my Swiss-American friend, Milly, that Corfu was the right spot to reflect and have some fun. And Corfu was steeped in history—written history going back to around 700 BC. That means ghosts, spirits, mostly neutral, but they are there. I saw things happen. At an ancient olive press once, I saw little children, maybe 4 to 6 years old, possessed by dancing spirits.

Suddenly, they began to dance and chant. They laughed and ran around, and then suddenly, they stopped. The people I was with said these kinds of harmless incidents happen a lot. And that's perfectly understandable given the history. As one gets used to being in such places, it becomes easier to accept the presence of parallel spirit worlds. And that is a good thing. And meeting Lucy was a gift. I spent my time with her and with my writing, and not an overkill of social activity. Among pitfalls of living in a small place are the constant tugs and temptation of intrigue, drama, gossip, and who is up to what. And that's fine for some people. In fact, some people have a real appetite for, and thrive on, those situations. Ah yes, they could be overheard in cafés in the morning just squawking away with the latest gossip.

You got some work done and recuperated?

Yes. I wrote several songs, a play called *The Bluesman*, and a scathing condemnation of Christian missionaries and Catholic education of indigenous peoples. In those days one could draw upon what they already knew, then go to a library for further research or interview. One can still do all of that, but today the internet has made research a lot less adventurous. I used to meet lovely ladies at the library back in the day. Even though they are supposed to be places of quiet, I used to pass a note to a lady as I walked by. That worked often for starting a conversation in the quiet zones.

And so, two months drifted by and I was feeling rested and energized. Lucy, tennis, writing, café lounging, visits to Julio's, an occasional party, and a few fun-filled evenings playing music at Club Med. That's how it went. Around mid-August Lucy decided that she wanted to return to Frankfurt, her hometown. She needed to regroup, make some decisions. Get serious, as she put it. That was certainly understandable. She was looking within, trying to discover more of herself, find direction. The last time I saw Lucy was as the Corfu port. Julio and I escorted her to bid farewell. Lucy shouted, "Bye my brothers!" from the deck of the ferry bound for Brindisi. That's the last time I saw her, or heard her voice.

Another chapter comes to a close?

That's what it was. It had been a great summer. As a result, I was in and out of Greece often over the next couple of years, having developed a few friendships, some lasting until this day. And there were special people like Margot Nichols, who more than once opened the doors to her homes in Corfu, and in Sainte-Romain near Beaune, for a period of recuperation from the madness and love of living.

Turning a page.

Turning like a mug! I had been in touch with friends in Denmark, as I wanted to go there and pay homage to some of the greatest musicians of all time, beacons of black music and beyond. Dexter

Gordon, Ben Webster, Kenny Drew, Jules Curtis; these cats and others were living in Copenhagen. I decided to head to Denmark before cold weather set in.

I know you got on a plane for Copenhagen. Everything else was up to the Cosmics. Tell us...?

I arrived in Copenhagen and checked into a decent hotel. Most hotels, regardless of price, are decent in Copenhagen. The next day, I got in touch with my friends, who I had met in Chicago a few years before. They were Danes that had studied at the University of Chicago. I was hoping that they could help me find a crib because I did not have money for too many nights in a hotel, no matter how inexpensive. As it turned out, they knew a lady that owned a huge house that she had divided into small apartments and rooms. The only drawback, they said, was the location. The house was in Vedbaek, about twenty kilometers from Copenhagen center. On the plus side, because it was outlying, the rent was cheaper.

It was a sunny September Sunday afternoon. We drove out of town and headed up the coast. To my right I could see towns across the bay, Malmo and suburbs. To my left were trees and wooded areas. The fall colors were already quite pronounced this far north. We arrived at a house in Tårbæk near Strandvejen. I was introduced to the lady who owned the property that had been recommended. I have forgotten her name, but we immediately liked each other. And she loved black music, blues and jazz. As it turned out, she and her late husband had travelled extensively in North and Sub-Saharan Africa and South America. There were artifacts throughout the home. Cushions from Morocco, masks, djembes, a kora, rugs– and headwear from Peru and Mexico. My soon-to-be landlady had lived an interesting life. She and her husband had at one time worked in the Danish Foreign Service. Their work involved extensive travel and sometimes a lengthy residency. After retirement, they continued to travel and add to their collection.

You were comfortable in her surroundings?

Absolutely. And she was comfortable with me. And after being introduced, and the pleasantries that followed, we got down to the business of finding a place for me to live. She asked none of the usual questions that would be asked by a white landlord of a black prospective tenant in the U.S. Her thing was: "Let's drive up to the house and see if you like it." She was this way because I had been introduced by mutual friends and racism was not at the core of her thinking. Providing me with a good home at a fair price is what was important for her.

And how was her place?

The house was at Strandvejen 335. My place was a large room, around 400 square feet, situated on the first floor of the divided house. I walked in and thought to myself that this is exactly what I needed at the time. There was no furniture, but the landlady said she could provide essentials, those being a bed, table, desk, and lamp. The kitchen and the bathrooms were communal, shared by all who lived there. There was a view of the courtyard, the Strandvejen, and the Strait of Øresund. She said the room was mine if I wanted it. I did, so we agreed on a price, and I paid for three months in advance to give me some breathing room as I learned the scene. . . the lay of the land. In the courtyard were a smaller one-bedroom house and a storage structure where my essentials were located. I didn't like the bed, so I bought a new one the following day.

Just like that, you have a crib. Are you ready for whatever?

I was ready. However, the only people that I knew were the friends from Chicago, so I really had to get around, especially since winter was not far off.

What about the other people in the house?

There were five others living there. They were cool people. One fellow was a bass player who I got along with; his place was next door to me. There were a couple of students upstairs, a young lady and young man. And, upstairs in a three-room configuration was Hannah, an attractive a single mother in her mid-twenties, and her son, Jacob, who was around six years old. I met Hannah the next day after moving in. Well, it wasn't a move-in, I just dropped my bags in the middle of the floor. Plop! Blam! Hannah offered to help me settle in. All the people in the house were very welcoming and offered to be of help.

What did she mean by settle in?

Hannah set about trying to give my place the feeling of being lived in. She brought a table cloth, candles, coat hangers, and other useful items. She brought extra pillows and a blanket. These kinds of things I would have had to go out and buy. Also, in the kitchen everyone used their own utensils. Hannah, being recently divorced or separated, had kept a lot from her old house and former life. On Tuesday evening, Hannah invited me to her place for dinner. Well, you know. . . dinner, wine, dimming of the lights, and Jacob with his aunt for some reason; the evening was proceeding as Hannah had imagined, I believe. Hannah and I became very good friends. We started hanging out upstairs and downstairs, and hanging out in Copenhagen listening to music. There wasn't much to do in Vedbæk as the landlady had said. In fact, it was downright boring. One good thing though, Hannah was head librarian at the music library in Holte, a town a few kilometers north of Vedbæk. LaBosse, this library had an incredible collection of jazz and blues, covering the beginning of sound-recording to the present. I spent a lot of time at the library and at home listening. Still, outside of the music, writing, walks by the sea, and hanging out with Hannah. . . to be home was to be bored. Of course, a remedy was playing music and spending time in Copenhagen.

How was the music scene?

I started checking out the scene after a couple of weeks. As is the case anywhere, one needs to find out the good leads for doing business, and what's a waste of time. The first time I went to the Jazzhus Montmartre, I met a drummer named Jules Curtiss and a painter, Bobby Jackson, I believe is his name. These cats were Montmartre regulars who knew the scene inside out. Bobby drove a big white Volvo station wagon, and he would often drive cats to gigs. He enjoyed doing that. One night, everybody that I wanted to meet was in the Montmartre plus another cat from Chicago, tenor sax player E. Parker Mc Dougal, who was founder of a groove called Chicago Hard Core Jazz. Bobby introduced me to John Tchicai, Ben Webster, Kenny Drew, and Dexter Gordon, and Niels-Henning Ørsted Pedersen, and others. I think it was the house band's gig, but everybody played some. But it wasn't no jam session– just seasoned cats dealing.

How did Bobby introduce you?

He said something like, "This is Beau, a young blues cat from

Chicago." Then you know, handshake, and so on. No big deal. So, I started coming to the Montmartre quite often. One night I was at a Ben Webster gig, and Ben asked me if I wanted to do a tune. I started thinking, Ben is a big-time, mellow swing master, and I'm coming out of a Chicago-style blues bag. But I do like to swing a bit. I called "Stormy Monday" and had Ben Webster kick off the tune, set the groove, tempo. Ben hit that intro: it worked. Then Dexter came up. Two verses, hit them with that harp, Ben's, Dexter's, and Neil's solos, closing verse. The audience loved it. I did that one tune and was able to pivot and get some gigs. But the most important thing about that tune was earning the respect of those I regarded as deities, through whom our ancestors spoke and future generations will continue to praise and honor. I felt that musically I would probably never be able to approach these cats. I mean I was twenty-two years old, just peeking into the book of life and possibilities.

That must have been damn heavy for you. Did the cats pick up on that?

I think they did. But you know, cats be cool. But I let them know that I was appreciative.

You say gigs started coming in?

Yes. The right people were at the Montmartre who also knew about my recordings with Archie Shepp. One guy worked in radio, and the other had a record store. Boom! University of Copenhagen, Jazz Club in Aarhus, and a music therapy gig in a mental institution. These gigs happened quickly and others soon followed. As a result of some money coming in I was able to get my wardrobe together. I had a couple of suits tailored at Brødrene Andersen, an exceptionally fine store.

Seems you're settling in. Any interesting twist and turns of excitement?

At first, I was excited by the number of willing women. I mean, I ain't going to get into numbers, but let me say this: after a while, and so many. . . boring. Well, there was one who turned out to be Hannah's cousin. She was a lot of fun and good people. The funny twist there was that she was engaged to a fellow from the Middle East who insisted on her remaining a virgin until marriage, which to my knowledge she did do. However, we did spend a lot of time to-

gether, and her alternatives to losing her virginity were nothing less than pure, unrestricted pleasure. I don't get those virgin guys, really.
Well that is literally twisting and turning. More?

Haha! One great thing that happened was when Duke Ellington came to Malmo, Sweden, across the strait. Ben Webster was a guest performer having a reunion with Duke. Bobby, Kenny Drew, and Dexter Gordon decided to drive to Malmo via the car ferry from Helsingør, Denmark, to Helsingborg, Sweden, then drive down. That meant they had to pass by my crib on Strandvejen. What a ride. I just sat and listened to those cats reminiscing. I mean, they touched on ladies, politics in the United States, Duke getting older, all kinds of topics and opinions. I remember Dexter was complaining about lack of legroom in the front. Kenny and I were in the back, and even though this model Volvo was considered a larger car, it was still tight. We got to the gig and man, I was in jazz paradise once again. Hanging with Duke, Ben, Kenny, Bobby, Duke's band. . . special! And the band was smokin', and Ben was in great form. And them cats introduced me as a music colleague, you know, and even though I was much younger, they didn't treat me as such. That felt good. I was one of the cats. A blues cat from Chicago.

Amazing people. Soul brothers! That's nurturing in the tradition of our Ancestors. Next?

As I said, it could be boring out in Vedbæk. The days were getting shorter, and the temperature colder. The people living in the house were disturbed if I came in after nine in the evening. It really annoyed them if I cooked something in the kitchen or played some music. One day Julio rang and told me about a party and concert at the Rainbow Music Hall in London. I headed to London on December 3, 1971, and went directly from Heathrow to the Rainbow in Finsbury Park. I hooked up with Julio and caught Freddie King and Leon Russell. Being in London was a major transition from dull-ass Vedbæk.

Do you still want to resume from 1971 in another volume?

Yes. We'll start that in Geneva, 1972, where I lived through some extremely trying times. I won't say too much now, but that is where I created the term *Eurosis*, because of all the deep psycho-dramas that were taking place in a society that represents itself as orderly and correct... Heidi and Hans in fairytale land, with accurate clocks. No way. I had never imagined such troubled people existed. That's when I started to look closer at Freud, Jung, J.A.C. Brown, and others. That's when the writings by Hesse and Mann took on new meaning for me. The European's battle for self-reliance versus religious reliance often manifested itself in behavior probably only understood by psychologists. Anyway, we'll move from Geneva, back to Corfu and Paris in 1973, back to adventures in Québec, and move on to Beverly Hills, Palm Springs, Wall Street, Senegal, Kenya, and so on. Fun and challenges.

Note: This conversation continues after photo section.

Photographs

Lincoln T. Beauchamp, Merida, Mexico, 1922

Betty and Lincoln Beauchamp, wedding day,
February 28, 1942, Little Rock, Arkansas

Betty Smith, circa 1930

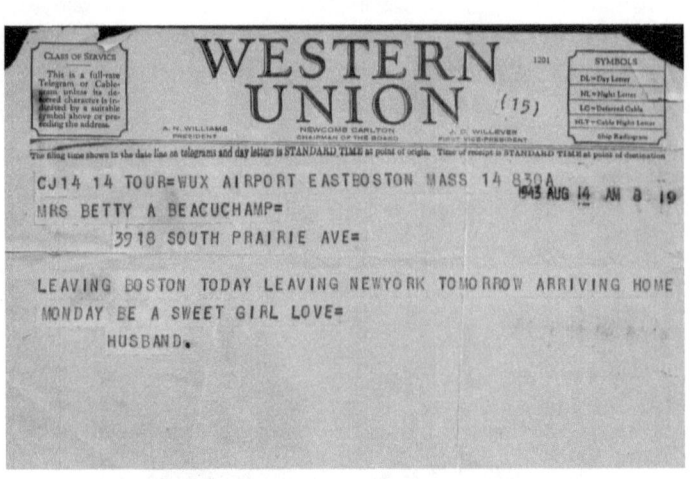

World War II days telegram to my mother, Betty, from my dad, who directed personell movement for the Navy.

With my sister, Margaret, right, 1951

Uncle Owsley and Betty Smith, my mother. Graduation day from Lincoln Institue, Lincoln Ridge, Kentucky, 1934. Diplomas in hand.

Smith Family in front of home. Harriet, mother, and James, father, front and center. Betty, my mother to the right of dad. Henderson, Kentucky, circa 1925

Family home, Independence Boulevard,
Chicago westside, 1962

With Julio Finn, right, Palmer Street, Cambridge, Mass, April 10, 1968

Amougies Music Festival, Amougies, Belgium, October, 1969

With Virgil W., left, and Mahadi W., right, Goree Island, Senegal, 1986

Jim Conley, alto and tenor saxophones; Memphis Slim, piano. Monte Carlo, Monaco, 1970

New Year's Eve, Theatre Ranelagh, Paris 1972

Standing: A.-C. McGraw; Margaret Beauchamp, my sister; me.
Seated: Daughter, Honoree Dakar; Lincoln Beauchamp, Sr., December, 1989

Linda Carter, center, with our daughter, Jessica, Toronto, 2014

Reunion with Archie Shepp, right. April Jazz, Espoo, Finland, 2007

With Eugene B. Redmond, left, Shaw's Crab House, Chicago, 1992

Standing, left to right: Famoudou Don Moye, Herb Walker, Roscoe Mitchell, Frank Lacy, James Carter, Malachi Favors Maghostut
Seated: Amina Claudine Meyers, Lester Bowie, Joseph Jarman, Chicago Beau. Art Ensemble of Chicago Tradition of Blues Tour, Rostock, Germany, 1993

With Johnny Griffin, left, Jazz Showcase, Chicago, circa 1993

With Beguine Beauchamp, daughter; and Dooney O'Neill Beauchamp.
Reykjavik Blues Festival, March 23, 2016

With Maya Angelou, ETA Cultural Arts Foundation, Chicago, 1991

Chicago Blues Experience Co-founders
Standing: Lincoln Beauchamp, Alex Rourke.
Seated: Tim Wright, Sona Wang, Bill Selonick.
December 18, 2011, Evanston, Illinois

Right now, you want to fast forward a few years to Chicago?

Yes, it's important to do so to bring clarity to my position on the Chicago blues scene, and to give our readers some insight on how some people and systems operate.

Where would you like to start?

I moved back to Chicago from Los Angeles with my wife and children on January 1, 1980. We moved into the Blackstone Hotel for a few weeks, which is where the world-renowned Jazz Showcase was located. That club was something special. Joe Segal, the owner, in my book did more for jazz as a club owner than anyone I can think of in Chicago. The main thing with Joe is respect for the music and musicians. Cats play the showcase from all over the world. Top cats and local cats. The Blackstone was a good spot to be in until we found an apartment, which we did eventually on Bittersweet Place on the North side.

You were new to the Chicago scene at that time?

Right. I hadn't lived in Chicago since 1967, since I was 18 years old. This is 1980: I'm turning 31 in February. I had no clue about the politics of the scene, the M.O. of club owners, nothing. I assumed that like most other places, the neo-colonial mentality of those that ran the music business was well intact. The reputations of unscrupulous promoters, record companies, club owners, booking agents, and others had been well documented. However, just how the Chicago scene operated was new to me, but it didn't take long for me to find out what the deal was, especially with certain individuals.

Who are you speaking about?

Well, I started checking out the clubs. B.L.U.E.S on Halsted Street was happening. It's still there—a small place with endless crowds. There was the Wise Fools over on Lincoln, and the Kingston Mines also on Lincoln. And a lot of other joints that came and went. On the South Side were the Checkerboard, Peppers, Theresa's, Palm Tavern, The Place, Brown's, and many more. And at this time Maxwell Street was still happening, and a few clubs on the West Side. The Regal Theatre was happening. There was music around, but the surge of the nineties hadn't hit yet. In the late eighties and nineties,blues clubs popped up everywhere. Kingston Mines was becoming known as a blues hotspot. I met the owner, Doc Pellegrino, who at that time seemed like a pretty decent fellow, who was convincing in his proclamation of being a lover and supporter of the blues. Now here's where I fucked up: I believed him. Partly because for the past few years I had been dealing with noble and honest people in almost every area of my life. I had been working as an investment broker in Beverly Hills for Rosenthal and Company, and at the time I met Pellegrino, I was working as a broker at the Chicago Board of Trade with Mercantile Trading Company. I had connections with money people, investors, and investment firm owners. One night I ran into Doc at B.L.U.E.S., and he told me that he was having difficulties, structural I believe, with the club. He said he had to move into a new place quickly. He needed money to temporarily move into the Galaxy Disco Nightclub, which was vacant. The man was convincing, and I was young and naive. I introduced Pellegrino to a group that I thought maybe could help him. Now, I've made a lot of deals with a handshake, from Chicago to Palermo, from Istanbul to Los Angeles. I ain't been screwed but once, and that was by Pellegrino. Our agreement by handshake was that I would receive a 5 percent commission for whatever amount of money I helped him find. I won't disclose the exact amount, but I'm still waiting on my 5 percent, thirty-five years later. He got the Galaxy opened which kept him in business until the current location on Halsted could be opened. At the time, I had a family, young kids at home, bills to pay. You know, an investment can go sour. One can lose everything. A business can fail. Entrepreneurs fail daily: some bounce back, some never. Some hit the super big time. Normally, I wouldn't speak about money affairs, but in this case, I'm talking about someone who claims to love black music, and who, by my own interaction with him, clearly has no like or respect for black people, and maybe not for musicians in general. They are a commodity– a tool to make a profit and to create cash flow. This is not about a failed endeavor or inability to pay back a loan. Those things are often and should be forgiven in certain circumstances. This is about a man who benefited greatly from my efforts and flatly refused to keep his word.

What reasons does he offer?

Lame bullshit. He said he thought I "did it for the blues." Is that crazy or what? If I did it for the blues, then I should really be getting paid. I was a man struggling, raising children. Is that the blues? This motherfucker is the classic plantation owner. He thinks he owns black musicians. And it's sad, pathetic to see so many veteran performers. . . legends— line up to play in his club. Here's a guy who takes in cash every single day. He's not a failed investor. He is a greedy, depraved, weasel-ass motherfucker. Dig this. He offered me drink tickets in his club for a couple of nights as compensation. This plantation-minded white man thinks that a drink or getting high is the common denominator that satisfies black people.

If you could describe Doc Pellegrino with one word, what word would that be?

Ignoble.

What about some of your other Chicago endeavors to get you established?

After the *Mines Affair,* I was quiet for a few years. I did have a column in a monthly music newspaper called *The Chicago Musicale*. I also travelled a bit in Kenya, and Senegal. In 1987 I started a literary magazine, *Literati Chicago*. My idea was to create a "Blues as Literature" environment in its pages. I see blues culture as the core element of black peoples' lives in bondage and decades of struggle since. Blues culture is many elements of Black survival throughout the African Diaspora. It includes theatre, filmmaking, poetry, literature, visual arts, crafts, musical instrument creations, inventions, music, and more. And it reflects social and economic injustices like discrimination, lack of employment and housing opportunity, unfair and prolonged incarceration of Blacks, police targeting of black males, and abuse of Black women. The blues is being stripped of African traditions and spirituality. The blues is spending a lifetime un-whitewashing oneself from centuries of being dis-Africanized. This is to say, rejecting quite logically the teachings of Christian missionaries and greedy preachers, who are just as guilty and wrong as Columbus. The blues is a rejection of all the others who've looted, raped, committed genocide, enslaved, and a lot more in the name of Christ and country, i.e., the ruthless, decadent, assholes who sat on the thrones of Europe.

The first issue of *Literati Chicago* came out in fall of 1988. It was well received. We, and when I say we, I mean me and my wife

at the time, A.C. McGraw, received good support from different areas of Chicago's creative and business communities.
Was that surprising?

No, it wasn't. The process of looking for support was defining, though. I mean, I approached people who made it clear that they wanted nothing to do with anything black, not even if they stood to profit. But I'm grateful to The Art Ensemble of Chicago and Famoudou Don Moye for their funding help, and also Bill Gilmore, RobHecko, and Pete Crawford, owners of B.L.U.E.S., Blues Etc., and all who, from the beginning, always had an advertising presence in my publications. Some people and organizations were overwhelming in their support. To name a few: the DuSable Museum, Paul Freeman and his Chicago Sinfonietta, Rizzoli Books, Guild Books, Nicole Smith, the State of Illinois, the City of Chicago, WFMT Radio, and Floyd Webb's Backlight Film Festival. Support came in many forms, from contributing writers to staff members. Many good people helped my vision of publishing a literary magazine become reality.

Did you gather momentum as a publisher after the first issue of Literati?

Interesting question because it has one of those yes and no answers. There was lots of interest from the literary community: we created a buzz. Submissions rolled into the mailbox daily. But the old problem was always present: money. We got grants and sold advertising. And my wife, A.-C., and I had a daughter, Honorée Dakar, born on January 17, 1988, the same month *Literati Chicago* made its debut at Rizzoli Bookstore in water Tower Place, and was circulated by Ingram Periodicals. But expenses far outweighed revenue. And we were criticized by certain snooty-ass, backwards thinking, not-for-profit minded people for selling advertising. Another thing was the technology was nowhere near what it is today for desktop publishing. In fact, *Literati* Number 1 was traditionally typeset. For A.-C. and me, this was all totally new. But it didn't take long to figure things out, to get on board with the latest technology available at that time. And you know, learning has its cost, and mistakes can be costly. We paid a lot of money for *Literati* Number 1, much more than necessary. Issue Number 2 cost quite a bit less, but I none-too-soon realized why universities, who have a constant source of funding, are the main publishers of literary magazines. So, after Number 2, I tried a different approach. I decided to create a glossy, large format magazine with certain writings translated into Italian. I called the new magazine *Literati Internazionale*, and I did it in collaboration with Southern Illinois University at Edwardsville. That was thanks to the efforts of Eugene B. Redmond, who was Poetry Editor, and Associate Publisher. SIUE paid a great deal of the expense, but they wanted to know what was done with the advertising money. They couldn't grasp that the magazine was a source of income for my family. I mean, other than my love for what I was doing, I had a fam-ily to feed. They just couldn't comprehend, and I wasn't telling them where my money was going on some form they sent me to fill out. *Literati Internazionale* was one stellar issue. I'm not the person who is going to comply with the demands of the school, especially since I gave them the idea. Again, because it was a literary review, they had difficulty understanding my idea about commercialization. I needed money, so I came up with another idea that I thought was urgently needed in the blues for the self-reliance of the culture of blues, as I explained earlier. I decided to combine blues, literature, lifestyle, and useful information for musicians, industry people, and fans in one magazine. I called it *The Original Chicago Blues Annual*—original because you-know-who tries to claim everything as theirs. I wanted to nail down the magazine's creator and ownership.

By far, OBCA was the best representation of blues culture in any print media. Conceived of, and produced by, a black person who is the Blues. And sadly, that's unique, because blues musicians are still seeking recognition and legitimacy from white people. I mean grown-ass black people, whose music is at the very core of modern music, are wanting to be authenticated and approved by Whites who have absolutely no connection with their history, pain, social, and economic conditions. Nothing! Interlopers!

It's a pity. My thinking is that no culture needs to be concerned about approval, ratings, and certification by those of another culture. That's why we had no record and performance reviews by the usual cadre of scribblers and charlatans who contribute their arrogance in blues magazines. In fact, there were never reviews, only recognition, praises, and blessings. Most of us want our creative efforts to be appreciated. But when you've been conditioned for centuries to believe that you must clear nearly everything with the Whites before it has any value, that is nothing less than self-loathing. Plantation colonial-minded white folks have played that against people of color and native peoples globally for centuries. My position with OCBA was, and still is; I don't give a fuck what Eurocentrism dictates—not about our music, dress, hairstyles, language, nothing. And everything I've just mentioned had been at some point denounced by them, and then eventually appropriated and profited from by them.

Can you imagine a Manchurian walking around Rome declaring what has value and what does not? Or a native of the Americas questioning the authenticity and quality of the art of Mali? But the Eurocentric mindset has judgment and classification for nearly everything. And they are kingmakers, crowning some persons that has nothing to do with the black blues experience as beacons of the blues. What arrogance! What stupidity! Janis Joplin, Paul Butterfield, Mike Bloomfield, Stevie Ray Vaughan, Gary Moore, John Mayall, and on and on. No doubt, these individuals are great artists who have respect for the Blues and its origins; however, they are not of the lineage of those whose experiences necessitated the creation, and evolution of the Blues.

Let me be perfectly clear here. There are blues people, some who happen to play music, and there are people who play and love the blues, structurally, poetically, and empathetically, but they are not blues people. They can never be. If they were, they'd be descendants of those who perished on plantations, in the seas, and in the rivers of Black blood and bones. They'd still be shaken by the thought of violated Black wombs. They'd be still reeling from the loss of children and parents on the auction block. They'd still be trying to rip away three hundred years of Christian whitewashing. They would gag at the memory of lynching and cross burnings. They would look in the mirror and love themselves even though they have been lightened by centuries of rape. They would openly venerate Malcolm X, Medgar Evers, Maya Angelou, Sterling Brown, Nelson Mandela, Trayvon Martin, Fred Hampton, Ida B. Wells, Mackandal, and on and on. They would hear in the distance, and in their brains incessantly, black mothers crying and black names ringing. The blues is history, the present, and the future. I know for sure that some heirs to economic and social hegemony truly love the blues as music and a distinct culture, but *being* the blues– that can never be.

You are right. I think outside of United States, there is much more appreciation for blues culture than within the United States.

That's true to an extent. Academically for sure, and there are diehard fans of black culture who are not pretending to be anything that they are not. Some of the greatest platforms for performance and study of blues and jazz are in Europe. Some of the best paydays are nearly anywhere outside of the U.S. A lot depends on who you are dealing with, and one's ability to deal. Remember, the ideas of exploitation, cultural cleansing, genocide, eugenics, Christian domination, Crusades, harsh punishment for so-called heresy and non-compliance are deeply rooted in Ancient Roman and Judeo-Christian societies. A great deal of that evil can be attributed to Constantine, the Catholic and Anglican Churches, and the menacing kingdoms of Europe and England.

Do you feel that you accomplished what you set out to do with your publishing venture?

Yes. From the first chapbook, *I The Blues*, published in 1987, to the coffee table book, *Great Black Music - The Art Ensemble of Chicago*, published in 1997, I'm pleased. There was never a lot of money to work with, but I managed. I published the works of over a hundred writers, poets, photographers, and artists. I feel fortunate to have had the honor to publish or republish some truly creative and inspiring writers and artists. People like Gwendolyn Brooks, Jayne Cortez, Amiri Baraka, Henry Miller, Deitra Farr, Pinkie Gordon Lane, Eugene B. Redmond, Henry Dumas, J. P. Donleavy, Hart LeRoy Bibbs, KalamuYa Salaam, Quincy Troupe, James Otis Williams, Mike Hennessey, Alejo Carpentier, Luis Rodriguez, David Witter, Floyd Webb, Isio Saba, Julie Parson Nesbit, Joan Hackett, Julio Finn, Preston Jackson, Barbara Barefield, David Whiteis, and scores more. And through interviews to have the thoughts shared of E. Parker McDougal, Paul Freeman, Johnny Shines, Alvin Singleton, Pinetop Perkins, Billy Boy Arnold, Junior Wells, Famoudou

Don Moye, Lester Bowie, Eddie Boyd, and others. LaBosse, this was a vision realized. Of course, in retrospect one can say I should have done this or that differently, but that's what growth is all about. Everything grows, in one direction or another, and hopefully, I'm growing for the better.

No regrets?

Not really. If anything comes close to a regret, it would be disappointment in the then Chicago Public Schools Superintendent, Ted Kimbrough. He committed to buying copies of *Literati Internazionale* for high school libraries. This cat had me come over to the CPS office on Pershing Road to drop of books and pick up a check. I get there, and some woman, a secretary or administrative assistant, I believe, is flipping the pages of *Literati Internazionale*. She tells me that the magazine is unfit for high school students. She points out a poem that has the word "fuck" in it and the back cover that featured a nude statuette by the renowned artist Preston Jackson. This woman was a total fucking non-intellect. A moron. Yet she convinced Kimbrough to renege on the purchase. I asked her about all of the nudes in European art—so -called classic Greek and Roman sculpture. She said that art was classic and was accepted at such, whereas the Jackson's work was not. What damn fools! Kimbrough and his art assessor. Pictures of some 3,000-year old naked statues of white people are okay, but the work of a well-respected black artist is not. A long way to go for some of us!

If I recall correctly, during your publishing period you were also involved in other endeavors, right

During that period, there was certainly a lot going on. In 1991 I founded Straight Ahead Productions, a company specializing in concerts, music production, publishing, advertising sales, and graphic design. I moved from an office that was basically a mailbox to one that was around 3,000 square feet at 213 W. Institute Place, in River North. Straight Ahead collaborated with an organization, Jazz in Sardegna, to co-produce festivals in 1992 and 1993. I brought in Chicago artists Jimmy Dawkins, Katherine Davis, Tommy McCracken, Deitra Farr, Shirley King, and others. Also, artists from Iceland were brought in. Halldor Bragason, founder of the fine Icelandic band Vinir Dora, brought his band to Sardegna along with the spectacular singer Andre Gylfadottir. Straight Ahead was involved with record production. I signed on with DIW Records Tokyo to produce a series of blues CDs for the company's GBW label. GBW means "Greetings From Blues World," which is how I greeted my Japanese partners once in a letter. They decided to use that as the name of the label. I produced nine CDs. Given the production budget limitations, I think a couple of them came out rather well, particularly those of Billy Branch and my own. But in way, more importantly, the artists got paid fair money. Nobody walked away complaining, as they often did with some Chicago labels. And a lot of that complaining was often to me, not up in the face of the persons they were complaining about, which is where it should have been. Anyway, I wanted to give the artists sizable advances, and DIW went along with that. I figured, get the artists as much as possible up front, because it can be a long wait to receive royalties, if ever. Plus, a lot of artists don't have a clue about accounting. Record companies can tell you anything– show you any kind of bullshit piece of paper with numbers. And some of the blues people were not equipped to question the numbers in a statement, if there was one. Anyway, out of that series there are recordings of Kay Reed, Valerie Wellington, Billy Branch, Junior Wells, Burning Chicago Blues Machine (which was Koko Taylor's band without Koko), and two by me. There is a live compilation recording that we called *Chicago Blues Night* that featured Deitra Farr, Jimmy Conley, Tommy McCracken, Katherine Davis, Willie Kent, Shun Kikuta, and me. There were also collaborations with my friend Halldor Bragason in Iceland. We brought in Jimmy Dawkins, Pinetop Perkins, Billy Boy Arnold, Shirley King, and Deitra Farr. Several recordings were made with Jimmy Dawkins, Pinetop Perkins, and Billy Boy Arnold. Without a doubt, Halldor and I were key in bringing the Blues to Iceland.

Straight Ahead was rolling. What else were you doing?

Besides running Straight Ahead, I was gigging quite a bit as well. I had lengthy tours in Poland, Italy, Iceland, and Germany during those years. I had many gigs with Jonas Blues Band, fine people and musicians from Rome. True believers. I also served on the Chicago Blues Festival Advisory Committee from 1987 until 1995, when I had already left Chicago. And I had my family which was always a priority. All and all, I was stretched pretty thin. I got pneumonia in 1992 just before the Sardegna Festivals. I was still recovering when I had to take on managing that situation with loads of unforeseen circumstances and unpredictable behavior by certain individuals. My assistant, Minka Maasdam, was a great help. Anytime you have a large group on the road, you must be in good shape all around. My brain was fine, but I was still weak from pneumonia, even though the sickness had left my body. But things were going along okay, as a company and individually. But you know, anyway you look at it, Straight Ahead was a small player in a business of millions. Survival is the key word.

Anyway, another thing that happened was that Valerie Wellington and I decided to form an organization that could serve the needs of blues artists. We called it The Chicago Blues Artists Coalition. The focus of the organization was healthcare, fair wages, education, family support, business counseling, event planning, fundraising, and more. We had nearly thirty musicians come to the first meeting. Now, Valerie Wellington, she was young and inexperienced when it came to understanding the nature of the club owner plantation mentality, and generally the nature of business. Chicago club owners claim ownership of the musicians who work regularly in their clubs. At that time there were several. I told Valerie the same thing I'm saying today: keep your business away from anybody that's in business on the Chicago blues scene. That means club owners, the record label owners, booking agents, promoters, and others. For musicians to coalesce is the last thing they want to happen. They have been exploiting musicians' lack of literacy, business sense, lack of self-confidence, and fear of reprisals for independent thinking for decades. I told Valerie, but she didn't listen. She didn't understand the nature of the beast. She wanted to have meetings at Rosa's Lounge, in my opinion, the belly of the beast. First meeting, lounge owner, Tony Mangiullo, was taking in all that transpired. In actuality, even though he provided the space, he should have not been present at the meeting. And I believe the only reason he was there, or offered his place for the meeting, was so that he could go and report back to the other club owners what was up. It hurts me to say this, one by one, tired-ass shuffling blues artists withdrew their interest in the coalition. Some of the Kingston Mines regular performers said that they had been warned by Doc Pellegrino that if they stayed in the coalition, they'd lose their jobs. Some other club owners told the musicians that they would take care of their needs; they didn't need to belong to any kind of organization. These meetings should have been held privately and completely away from the people you going to try to negotiate with. I said it then, and I'm saying it now. Keep your business secret in Chicago until the time is right, and only release info through official channels that are part of your team.

That's a shame– that blues people just were not ready for, and lacked the courage to, bring about a change.

Exactly. And we had good media coverage. George Papajohn at the *Chicago Tribune* did a great story, as did *Ebony* magazine. But fear is a motherfucker. The syndicate of blues business people struck fear in the hearts of some of Chicago's blues people with the same old tactic used to prevent slave revolts: turn us against each other. The collective imaginations of those against the coalition couldn't envision how they could benefit. I think that a successful Blues organization could be a benefit to everyone involved because the more people you reach, the greater the possibility for new business and expansion across the board.

I know you wanted to cover some recent history before we close out Book 1. In closing, is there anything you'd like to share?

Yes. I left Chicago and went to Montreal in September of 1994. My wife and I had been separated since September of 1992. She moved with our daughter to North Carolina. I hated to see that. I mean, I ruled out North Carolina as a place to live, and that pain cut deeply because my daughter was there. I wish it had been possible for her to have lived elsewhere with me. I wasn't going to live under no southern yoke, or any other for that matter. I felt that I had made a positive contribution to black blues culture in Chicago and beyond. I was fatigued. Also, I deeply felt that nothing in the social and economic order of Chicago could ever change. That made my decision to live elsewhere easy. I spent nearly two years in Montreal, then moved to Italy. The first six months were spent nearly in total seclusion in Tuscany. I rented a small two-bedroom house with a frog pond and lots of land in a verdant valley near the village of Boccheggiano, which is situated between Massa Maritima and Siena. For weeks at a time the only people I spoke with were Adamo, the gardener; the shopkeepers in the village; and Tito the postman, who turned out to be a blues-loving guitarist. Tito lived in Massa Marittima and organized music festivals. We have been friends since those days. My Tuscany evenings were consumed with reading, writing, music, and listening to the nightly gnarling and grunting of roaming packs of *chingali*.

My father died in November of 1996. I went to see him in Chicago about two weeks before his passing, and stayed another two weeks afterwards looking after his affairs along with my sister. Going through the effects of a person who had a fifty-plus years law practice was all consuming and overwhelmingly interesting. There was even a good laugh that happened. We found hidden among his old files a magazine called *Chunky Asses*.

Chunky Asses!

Yeah, the same one that can be seen in the Eddie Murphy movie, *The Golden Child*, in the newsstand scene. I cracked up when I saw this. I mean I'm definitely a booty man, and so was my Dad. I guess it's in the genes. Thank you, Daddy! Shortly after my return to Italy, I was compelled to end my seclusion for economic reasons. I moved to Rome. While living in Italy, I married for the fourth time. My wife, Dooney, and her two sons, Luca and Raffy, and I moved to Loule, Portugal, in the Algarve in April 2001. Another adventure in existing ensued. In 2003, Dooney gave birth to our daughter, Beguine. In January 2005, we relocated to LaGrange Park, Illinois. For the next few years I maintained a low profile in the Chicago area, but was quite active in Europe. Nothing had changed in Chicago. In fact, from a blues musicians' business perspective, things had gotten worse.

In 2011, I came up with the idea for an ultra-high-tech, interactive blues museum for Chicago. I found partners and we co-founded the Chicago Blues Experience. Keep your eye on the newspapers!

LaBosse, my friend and brother, thanks for working with me the past three years to bring my recollections to these pages.

Any words to close-out?

Yes. To young people I say, explore, dream, engage the world. Every generation says, "Be careful, the world isn't what it used to be." That's true. One has to adjust to the world they are in, and try to influence it in a positive way whenever possible. And never stop learning, giving, and loving. That starts at home.
Beau, thanks for the honor. Let's uncork some Champagne. Praises and Blessings.
 Praises and Blessings. May the Ancestors be Honored.
Ashé

To be continued.

www.ingramcontent.com/pod-product-compliance
Lightning Source LLC
Chambersburg PA
CBHW020650300426
44112CB00007B/316